More Praise for This Book

"Finally, an instructor who actually demonstrates what he presents to the group as best practices. Jonathan's fervor for training is as prevalent in the classroom as it is in *Confessions of a Corporate Trainer*."
—*Wayne P. St.Louis, CSM, USA retired, Lead Associate, Booz Allen Hamilton*

"Jonathan Halls' *Confessions of a Corporate Trainer* provides a real look at what corporate trainers should be focused on. It's an inside look that will prompt thought and reflection and provide practical tips that help make anyone a better trainer."
—*Matthew Pierce, Learning and Video Ambassador, TechSmith Corporation*

"After working with nearly 1,000 corporate trainers, I can attest that *Confessions of a Corporate Trainer* provides a vivid and authentic peek behind the curtain for the world of professional trainers. The stories within the book brought back many memories and Halls's practical steps for continuous improvement are applicable for any trainer, regardless of experience."
—*Dean Griess, Director of Learning Delivery at a Financial Institution*

"*Confessions of a Corporate Trainer* is an invaluable tool for anyone wanting to transform themselves from a professional trainer to a training professional. Jonathan Halls rips off the veil, exposing the guts of the training world and they are crystal clear."
—*Jeff Sinclair, Senior Manager of Training and Talent Development, Sunrun*

"Jonathan's look at the world of training is both entertaining and insightful. Filled with honest stories about what the life of a trainer is really like, this book shares practical advice on the true challenges of this field and how you can overcome them."
—*Bianca Woods, Senior Manager of Programming, The eLearning Guild*

"I've spent nine years as an instructor and course designer in the military. *Confessions of a Corporate Trainer* highlights how Jonathan Halls is revolutionizing the process of delivering quality instruction and design."
—*Sean Lawler, CPO, U.S. Coast Guard*

~~THE LIFE~~

CONFESSIONS

OF A

CORPORATE

TRAINER

AN INSIDER TELLS ALL

JONATHAN HALLS

atd
PRESS

ATD Press is an internationally renowned source of insightful and practical information on talent development, training, and professional development.

ATD Press
1640 King Street
Alexandria, VA 22314 USA

Ordering information: Books published by ATD Press can be purchased by visiting ATD's website at www.td.org/books or by calling 800.628.2783 or 703.683.8100.

Library of Congress Control Number: 2019934393

ISBN-10: 1-947308-92-0
ISBN-13: 978-1-947308-92-3
e-ISBN: 978-1-947308-93-0

ATD Press Editorial Staff
Director: Sarah Halgas
Manager: Melissa Jones
Community of Practice Manager, Learning & Development: Amanda Smith
Developmental Editor: Jack Harlow
Associate Editor: Caroline Coppel
Text Design: Michelle Jose
Cover Design and Illustration: Faceout Studio, Spencer Fuller

Printed by Versa Press, East Peoria, IL

For the people who have attended my train-the-trainer and advanced trainer programs over the past two decades. You have taught me much, shaped my practice, and are responsible for my success today.

CONTENTS

PREFACE

A FEW YEARS AGO, I was at an event for learning professionals, somewhere in North America. I won't tell you where in case I incriminate myself. Not seeing anyone I knew, I joined a group near the drinks counter who were shooting the breeze about their work. In particular, how to deliver a good training session.

"You need to check the classroom the night before, to ensure tables are set up in the right order," one guy said proudly. I later found out he'd been a trainer for just over six months. Another said, "It's critical to arrange the tables in your room so there's space for you to perform. I mean, a lot of training is acting, right?" He was one of those engaging types with a loud voice and everyone nodded their heads. "Oh, yeah," a third chimed in, "the successful trainer needs to own the room."

The conversation felt like deja vu. Because it could have been a word-for-word re-enactment of a conversation that I'd heard at another conference the month before. In fact, it's a conversation I've heard many times around the globe. In Europe, the Middle East, and North America. At conferences or in staff meetings of training departments.

Universal Collective Set of Rules

Over my years of experience, I've come to notice a universal set of dos and don'ts that exists within the collective consciousness of the training profession. There's no central repository where it's written down but it's like an oral constitution that somehow everyone knows. "Call participants before class for an informal needs analysis." Or, "Check participants' learning styles and adjust your instructional plan." Then, "Never start a class late—it disrespects the folks who arrive on time." And, "Dress one level above the participants."

You won't just hear trainers reciting these collective rules. The web is littered with blog posts that posit these rules under headings like "5 Things Awesome Trainers Do" or "Dos and Don'ts of Training." But what if you can't follow them? Or if you don't want to?

For example, many trainers fly into a city at 7 p.m. the night before a class, after the facility is closed, and have no chance of checking the room they'll be in. If the class is being held at a hotel, the room may be booked for an event that evening. And how about calling participants before class? Noble in theory unless you lead four classes a week with 20 participants. Does any trainer have time to call 80 people a week and talk for five minutes? In fact, do participants have time or even the desire to play along?

Universal rules often sound great in theory. In this case, some are fine but often they're impractical. There is reason to question their utility from a learning perspective.

Too Much Pressure

I work with learning professionals around the globe in my train-the-trainer programs, professional development workshops, and coaching. And I get the sense many invest valuable time and energy trying to be the shiny happy trainer who follows the universal rules. Adhering to the rules is a huge burden. Some feel that if they don't follow these rules or techniques they'll become a bad trainer. Others nurse a sense of guilt, worrying that if they don't they're committing professional malpractice. And those who intentionally ignore them because they think there's a better way don't have the guts to tell anyone because they'll hear from peers, "Aww gee, you're not supposed to do that."

Well, I want to tell you something. It's impossible to be a truly *transformative* trainer, who gets real results, while living up to this universal collective set of rules for training.

A Book of Confessions

This leads me to my first confession of many in this book. I break more of these universal training rules in my practice as a workplace learning professional than I follow. I do so carefully and deliberately, of course, making sure that breaking them is not unethical or unprofessional. I've discovered that the less I'm tied down by these unwritten rules, the more I feel free to truly help people learn. And interestingly, I've seen increased feedback scores because I'm focused on the learners, not on my performance as a trainer.

Many of the universal rules are more about how we as trainers perform than how we help learners build their skills and knowledge. I mean, who cares if there's space at the front of the room for me to perform—it's not meant to be my show, it's the learners'. Who cares whether I dress one level above the learner or not—so long as I have a shower and don't smell in the classroom or wear clothing that's offensive, that should be alright.

Now some of this talk may be uncomfortable. I get that. If you're a big fan of learning styles, and you read how much I think they're misleading because of the research refuting them, that may be disconcerting. As you work your way through these pages, you may find that while some things resonate, others make you sit back and think, "I don't and can't agree." That's fine! Diversity of ideas and seeing other perspectives is what leads to richer understanding. But I share my stories and questions respectfully, hoping they'll encourage the work you do and give you the confidence to also question some of what you might be doing on automatic pilot and the assumptions you make about your work.

Throughout this book, and indeed in the title, I use the term *trainer.* You'll recall that the industry has referred to the role of the trainer with different words over the years. *Instructor, teacher, coach, facilitator, workplace learning professional,* and *talent specialist* are just a few I can immediately recall. These words are helpful to our profession in understanding what we do, but to anyone outside the talent world, they don't mean a whole lot. Use the term trainer, though, and most people get it. So, in this book I'm sticking to the term most people know, using it to mean facilitating, teaching, coaching, and anything else we do to help learners do the work of learning in today's organizations.

While a lot of what I say is couched informally, sometimes with humor, everything I say is driven by a real passion for the work you and I as trainers do to help people and organizations. I truly believe it's a noble thing to be a trainer. We help people do the work of making themselves more skillful and knowledgeable. These new or deeper skills and knowledge help organizations function better and create value for their stakeholders. In government, that value goes to citizens and community members through public services. In commercial organizations, the value goes to owners or shareholders whether they be an individual in Nebraska or a retirement fund supporting your grandparents in Florida. For nonprofit organizations, the value goes to people in need around the world, whether it's helping to eradicate malaria in Angola or support microenterprises in Bangladesh businesses. Yes, what we do is noble when exercised professionally and ethically. But with it comes an enormous privilege. When you facilitate a webinar, lead a face-to-face class, or create content such as a video or instructional podcast, learners open their minds and allow you to influence their thinking. This is awesome and as such requires us to do everything we can to be great trainers. That's at the heart of this book.

What's in This Book

What can you expect over following pages? I want to explore what it really means to be a successful trainer in all its gritty reality. Not to prepare you for the circle of conversation at a conference where trainers talk about the dos and don'ts of our work. But to support you, as a reflective practitioner, to continually deepen the learning experience for the people you serve as a trainer. How are we going to do it?

Leading off, I confess that no matter how well we plan a learning experience, its success is never really guaranteed. In chapter 1, I share a story about something that happened to me in Moscow.

To know which of the unwritten rules to break, we need a research-based understanding of learning in the workplace. Chapter 2 explores what that is.

Have you ever noticed that some of your best performances are when you aren't trying to perform? Chapter 3 covers the power of shifting your focus from how you perform to how the learner gets to practice.

While trainers work to help the organization, it's the leaders of the organization who hire and fire us. Chapter 4 reviews what this means for our work, how we align it to the business, and how we handle the many conflicting priorities we face.

In many training departments, tension develops between instructional designers and trainers. It doesn't have to be this way. Chapter 5 provides advice on how to leverage the richness this relationship brings.

It might just be me, but I find myself dumping my training plan once I'm on site as often as I end up following it. And I don't think that's a bad thing. Chapter 6 delves into why that may be good in your own practice.

Effective learning reaches way beyond the training room. It's incumbent on us to ensure the learning extends from the classroom into the workplace and all its influences. Chapter 7 takes us through the jungle of the learning ecosystem.

What do you do when most people have only poor impressions of training? These lasting images mean we must also assume the mantle of ambassador for talent. Chapter 8 considers how we can solve this problem with stories.

Whether you're in the classroom or in front of a computer screen all day, in the office, at home, or on the road, one critical topic we don't talk enough about is energy management. Trainers juggle massive workloads and often feel like it's impossible to keep up. Chapter 9 explores strategies to combat this.

If you are on the road a lot, it's important to be honest about one aspect of a trainer's life that many hate: travel. Chapter 10 offers ways to make travel and hotel stays less miserable.

Not unlike other fields, the training profession is full of hot air and buzzwords. Keeping current can be confusing because every year there's a new wave on enthusiasm about something different. Chapter 11 proposes turning to learning science, with a critical eye, to stay on top.

The future changes more rapidly every year, and this will continue to have a big impact on trainers. Chapter 12 looks at the key skills we need to stay competitive in the world of artificial intelligence, robots, and other uncertainties.

ACKNOWLEDGMENTS

I DELIVERED MY FIRST EVER training session in 1987. It was a six-part class on broadcasting at the local public radio station where I volunteered at as a kid. I was still in high school. You could say I started writing this book back then, when I discovered how to share learning with a small group of radio enthusiasts. I've been gathering material for this book through my work as a media trainer, learning executive, leadership trainer, small training business owner, and university student. It's 30 years in the making.

For this book, I decided to share stories about my life as a trainer. But I'm not the only one with interesting experiences. I'm honored that some trainers I hold in high regard have agreed to write sidebars about challenges they've faced as trainers and how they overcame them. You may recognize some of their names—many have written books about training sitting on your bookshelf. Others are tireless workers in organizations where they work to help people. Thanks to my good friend, Elaine Biech, whose very long list of books has influenced our profession for decades. And authors Lou Russell, Halelly Azulay, and Cindy Huggett, all thought leaders in our profession. And thanks Wesley

Anderson—a reflective practitioner who always makes me think. I'm touched and grateful that these folks have shared their stories. It goes without saying that the fact they were kind enough to do so does not imply they necessarily agree with everything I've written in this book.

Above all, what I hope is that as you read, you'll find similarities or familiar threads in our stories with your own. After all, trainers go through similar ups and downs whether you work for an insurance company or on the factory floor.

In addition, a lot of people knowingly and unknowingly contributed to this book. The late Alex Vale inspired me to pursue adult education, which makes me one of the unusual folks who is not an accidental trainer. Alex's influence helped me see my future work back in the late 1980s. Mike Newman was a professor at the college where I got my adult education degrees in the 1990s. He demonstrated through his practice what facilitating learning was really about, inspiring a fascination for Paulo Freire. At the BBC, Charmaine De Souza, who took a big risk in hiring this unknown broadcast trainer from Australia, modeled professional training management and how to align training to business goals. And the trainers I worked with at the BBC—wow—I'm still awestruck by their skills and professionalism. And the late Madeline Finnerty was a wise collaborator, too, who influenced a lot of my thinking.

The folks who run ATD's Education Department have also been an important part of my professional development over the years. Linda David, Courtney Vital, Elizabeth Hannah, Alicia Cipriani, Vanessa Fludd, Shana Campbell, Eliza Auckerman, and Bettina Wolf. I know I've forgotten some—forgive me. But thank you friends. And there's a list too long to publish who also taught me an incredible amount of stuff about training and about myself. These are the folks who have attended workshops I have facilitated around the globe. I consider you all my teachers. Some of these folks as well as a number of clients pop up throughout the book. However, in a small number of circumstances, I have changed names, geography, and other identifying details to protect their privacy.

But it's not just training folks who helped me write this book. I couldn't have done any of this without the support of my favorite person in the world: my wife, Sharon. She's the one who puts up with me being grumpy when it takes me longer than I plan to write a chapter. Who doesn't make any snarky comment when I bring my manuscript on vacation to work on, even though I promised I wouldn't work. And doesn't put demands on me when I cloister myself in my office to pound the keys on my keyboard. That big smile and encouraging manner is the fuel that enables me to complete the task.

Finally, I want to send a shout out to the ATD book folks who let this project go ahead. It started, like two of my books, over lunch with Justin Brusino. We both like burgers and French fries. "Do you have another book in you?" he asked. "Yeah, but you won't publish it." "Why not?" "Because it's going to be written in first person and I want some space to poke fun at the profession." "Try me," he said. He was either courageous or sleep deprived, tending to his young son, because he said, "Let's give it a shot." This is probably a risky book for ATD Press because it's not in their normal mold. It's not an instructional volume like much in their catalogue. They let me be a little wild. So, thanks ATD for your faith in me. Amanda Smith took up oversight and put me in the capable hands of Jack Harlow who also edited my last book. Jack's been an amazing editor because he has helped me tone down some of the chapters when I got too excited. And challenged some of my ideas helping me improve them. He's been incredibly tolerant of me missing deadlines and working around my hectic travel schedule.

This book belongs to all these people who have helped over the past 30 years.

1

THE MYTH OF THE SHINY HAPPY TRAINER

Smooth seas do not make skillful sailors.
—African Proverb

You've got to be kidding, I thought to myself. *Did that guy just walk out?* Every trainer has a list of what they don't want to have happen in a classroom. A participant storming out was near the top of mine.

He was tall, mid-40s, with bushy eyebrows and a gray beard. He was sitting in the middle of the classroom and in all honesty, I hadn't really noticed him until then. Now, I'll never forget him. We were two hours in—25 participants and me—cocooned in a dingy Moscow classroom.

I had begun explaining the theory of interaction when he pushed back his chair, dragging its feet across the cold, tiled floor, and stood up. Hastily pulling on an overcoat—one of those thick, heavy ones that you see in spy movies set during the Cold War—he stomped out, muttering a string of Russian words that hung in the air like a bad smell. I had no idea what he'd said, but everyone looked at me.

Crap. Was this really happening? I must have looked so dumb, standing there in front of 24 people.

Shiny Happy Trainers

I bet you've been to training sessions with amazing trainers who come across as consummate professionals. They're polished, confident, unflappable. They stand in front of the class, using the right facial expressions, looking genuine, and carefully managing each inflection. They pull from their arsenal of nonverbal expressions such as the occasional furrowed brow to make you feel as if you've said something profound—that they hadn't considered until that moment. I have three trainers in mind, and while I can't recall what they were teaching, I remember being blown away by their incredible stage presence.

I have a term for these trainers: *shiny happy trainers,* from the 1991 song by R.E.M., "Shiny Happy People."

At that moment in Moscow, I was not a shiny happy trainer.

Moscow is not at its best in November. Sure, it can be pretty in the summer. But at about the same time the air becomes crisp and the leaves turn red in the northern states of America, Moscow goes gray, dirty, and muddy. Even freshly fallen snow has a gray pallor. If someone had said two weeks before that class that I'd be in Russia, I would have laughed and ordered another drink. But here I was with the bearded guy. Or more accurately, without him.

My mistake was picking up the phone. It was a desperate call two weeks ago from Gerhard in Frankfurt.

I Got That Queasy Feeling

"Ekhard pulled out of the Moscow gig. Can you do his workshop?" Ekhard was a genial German professor who, like me, ran digital storytelling workshops for journalists. He wasn't the type of trainer to bail just two weeks before an event. "It's just a workshop on digital storytelling, like the one you did in France" Gerhard had said. "Nothing taxing, just wing it—it's so easy, you can do it in your sleep."

So easy, you can do it in your sleep. I get a queasy feeling when people tell me something is easy. That statement and its siblings "I've got a slide deck; just ad-lib against my bullet points" and "Don't sweat the details; just be yourself" should set off alarm bells for any trainer. Our instinct should be to run fast from these requests, because there's no such thing as easy when it comes to training. Just throwing things together is not sufficient.

So I started to say no. I'm a trainer, after all! *I don't just throw things together,* I thought, feeling like a shiny happy trainer. I do things right. I start with a needs analysis. I identify the client's goals, learn about their company, and determine the participants' skill and experience levels. Then I design exercises and create worksheets to help participants learn skills that assist them in their work. Preparation doesn't just happen overnight. Nor does booking travel or standing in line at the embassy so a bureaucrat can stamp a visa in my passport.

But the reality is, trainers are often called to deliver training at the last minute. In many organizations, training is the last thing people think of—such as when IT asks you, "We're rolling out new software to 500 users next week. Can you train them, please?" Disorganization isn't always the cause of last-minute requests. Maybe a key player leaves the team or drops out, as with Ekhard. In most cases, trainers should say no, but many have no choice. For me, my largest client was in a bind, and it was an important workshop. "No" wasn't an option.

With some hesitation, I finally agreed, telling him I wasn't going to "wing it" but would instead follow a rapid instructional systems design process. He put me in touch with Sergei in Russia to get the needs analysis going. It turned out that Sergei wanted a different focus on digital storytelling than the one I had given in the France workshop. With that in mind, I designed the session, planned exercises, and created worksheets, thinking that I'd accounted for every hypothetical.

Despite the short turnaround, I was feeling confident. Plus, I'd finally get to work in Russia. I'd grown up reading so many spy novels in the 1980s that Russia had this magical hold over my imagination. Add to that, this was back when I lived in the UK, and I was always excited by the prospect of travel to a country I'd never been before. A few days' work in Moscow would be that adventure and provide serious bragging rights at London cocktail parties—how many people did I know who had worked in Russia? "When I was in Russia . . ." I could start.

Except now I know that this story wasn't meant to be one to boast about.

Crimson Red

As the echo of his footsteps and clunk of the door closing died out, silence fell over the room, and his departure sank in, I experienced what many trainers feel when something goes wrong: guilt. It was my fault. And then I stood there like a deer in the headlights, imagining shiny happy trainers who never had participants storm out of their classroom. And even if that *did* happen, they would react with poise. Look self-assured and smile. Crack jokes and have participants eating out of the palm of their hand. They would know how to get the class back on track.

With slumped shoulders and my heart pounding loud against my chest, I ran through what I could do to salvage the sinking class. I'd led train-the-trainer programs and read plenty of books on the dos and don'ts of being a good trainer. Was I talking too fast? I could slow down. Did I say something that was culturally insensitive? That might be harder to fix. For what felt like an eternity, my brain fired questions at me, trying to prevent me from being a dull grumpy trainer. (In reality, it was maybe 10 seconds.) Then I stopped: Maybe I was getting all this wrong. He may have just needed to go to the restroom. Perhaps the Russian words he uttered on his way out were, "Man, I gotta go to the men's room—age, you know."

I took a deep breath and moved to the next slide. And four more folks shuffled out.

Perhaps you've had this experience: Something goes wrong and all eyes are on you. A product you're demonstrating fails. Or a disruptive participant disputes your slide deck. In a flash, your world slows down. You feel clammy, and you lose your ability to speak eloquently. Words tumble out in staccato fashion—sometimes you even say something you later regret.

Welcome to what I call the great limbic shutdown, in which our brain's limbic system catapults us into fight or flight mode. Some call it the amygdala hijack—our status is threatened, and we lose our sense of control. My normally pale face went crimson red. But I took a deep breath and managed to summon enough false confidence to suggest that the class take a break. As the remaining 15 participants headed for coffee, Sergei, who had been standing nervously at the door, scrambled across the room in a panic. I looked down and saw that my hand had started to shake. As he neared the front of the room, I put on a brave face and faked a smile.

"Everything going OK, Sergei?"

Keep Calm and Carry On

Sergei was standing next to me at the front of the now empty classroom. With a pained expression he put his hand on my shoulder and asked, "Can you teach digital revenue streams?"

"Huh?" I said. He paused, looked at the floor, and said in a low voice, "We advertised this as a workshop on digital revenue streams."

TRAINER ANGST

Trainers face many uncertainties when they walk into a room of people they've never met. For all our bravado, we often harbor insecurities that undermine our ability to be focused and deliberate. I call it "trainer angst." Sometimes it stems from a lack of experience or the simple fear that we're not great presenters. Or worse, we worry that people won't like us and will write nasty things on evaluation sheets.

No one likes trainer angst; in fact, a lot of trainers pretend it doesn't exist. But many who do admit to it have told me that they are worried about "being found out." I've certainly felt that way when running a workshop on content I'm not as familiar with as I would like. To compensate, some trainers generate overconfidence, which creates considerable nervous tension and a less-than-genuine learning experience for participants. Others feel so nervous before a class that they manage only a few hours of sleep. I was one of them once. Even now, I occasionally find myself tossing and turning the night before I conduct a workshop full of people I don't know.

Overconfidence can manifest in many ways. Sometimes it's self-congratulatory talk, other times false humility, and still other times throwing around buzzwords and obsessing over the latest fad. Some folks deal with it by attempting to exert more control over the class through insane amounts of preparation or by imposing overbearing rules in class, such as, "Talk only when you have the magic ball" or "No cell phones allowed in class."

There's no perfect way to get rid of trainer's angst. For some, it simply takes time—the more you train, the more comfortable you become with the inherent uncertainty every new class brings. And be in no doubt: Delivering learning is unpredictable and messy. You rarely know ahead of time the hidden agendas, expectations, experience levels, and energy that different participants will bring to the classroom. Success for the seasoned trainer is less about how well they deliver the content than how they draw on these competing dynamics to direct people to the learning objective.

No kidding. And I was the doofus teaching them digital storytelling.

What had been the point of the two phone conversations I'd had with Sergei, running through the learning objectives and tweaking them for his participants? And how about the hours I spent administering the needs assessment? And the two days tailoring the session and creating worksheets based on this needs analysis? How did this all happen?

They say that when you have lemons, you should turn them into lemonade. That phrase was probably coined by a perpetually happy person who sees every glass as half full—someone who'd make a terrific shiny happy trainer. Because this situation had a bitter taste, and it wasn't going away.

After the break, I was able to transition from storytelling to revenue streams. I stuttered and stammered through a lot of it because while I knew enough of the topic to get by at a high level, I had never taught it at the depth that these learners required. While I had participants doing exercises, I was online doing research and emailing colleagues for deeper insights I could add. I had no quippy little stories, charm, or charisma. I just plodded through the topic, at a pace slow enough for me to figure out the next half hour while they did an exercise, and fast enough for them to think I had planned it that way.

Trainers are not supposed to admit things like this. I'm a professional, after all. But I had no choice, and at least after the break, 15 people came back, not demanding a refund. I'd come to this with good intentions and done lots of planning, but because of the communication failure, I had to dump everything I prepared and make it up as we went along.

Isn't there a rule book for trainers somewhere that says if you don't know the answer, don't pretend you do? Well, sometimes it's not always as straightforward. I'm not suggesting deception, but how would it have gone if I'd stood up and said, "They hired me to teach storytelling, but told you I was going to teach revenue streams. I'm not prepared for revenue streams—in fact, it actually bores me because I teach storytelling. So while they will still take your registration money, and sure as heck pay me for my efforts, I'm going to wing it and teach you something I don't like and am only a partial expert on. It'll be a great day, but most of the time, I'll be two pages in front of you." Yeah, try that.

Afterward, in a Georgian restaurant, Sergei apologized profusely. But nothing in that lemon of a workshop turned into lemonade. It was physically and mentally exhausting. More things went wrong on that trip where I had to cover for other people's mistakes, but I'll tell you about them in the sequel. To this day, my wife remarks on how I arrived home looking like a ghost. I'd gone straight from Heathrow Airport to some American friends in Bayswater for Thanksgiving, and I walked in the door pale and drained.

Most trainers have tough assignments like this—in fact, you're probably having nasty memories as you read this story. Such is the life of a trainer. But what had gone wrong? I was mad with Gerhard and Sergei. I was angry that I'd been put in a position where I'd stand in front of people and look like an idiot.

Silver Lining

Despite this grueling experience, Moscow clouds have a silver lining. Sergei arranged a tour guide to show me around before I flew home. My guide, Christina, then in her mid-70s, had been a translator for the Soviet propaganda apparatus and introduced me to Russia in a way only a local could. It was incredible—I learned from someone who had lived in Soviet culture and seen all the changes. She gave me a firsthand account of Glasnost and Perestroika—the two defining political pushes at the end of the Soviet era—that corrected my naive understanding gleaned from superficial Western media accounts.

The most exciting part of the tour was when Christina told me she had witnessed a decisive event in history. In May 1972, she was sitting on a bus with other translators waiting for their assignments when a KGB agent—no doubt wearing the kind of overcoat they wore in spy films—climbed aboard, pointed to her, and ordered her to follow him. Moments later, she was translating the social conversation between President Brezhnev and President Nixon. What an amazing experience spending time with walking history.

Being a trainer can be taxing. But it can also expose you to incredible experiences that change the way you see life. In just a few hours, I had learned more about Russian history and culture than I had in six years of high school. Probably worth the anguish of the past few days.

A few weeks later, still mad about the Moscow session, I got some participant feedback. To my disbelief, the session received great feedback, though less surprisingly the first few hours were described as too slow. Most interesting was that they got much more out of the workshop than I thought possible. When people want to learn, they learn. There's something amazing about the learning process. Often it takes years to appreciate how much it really is about them rather than us. It's tempting to think that learners' success comes down to what we do, but in reality, it's more about what they do.

The Agile Trainer

The fact that those people stormed out of my class was probably a good thing, because every experience offers an opportunity to learn. The tougher the experience, the deeper the learning. As the African proverb suggests, smooth seas do not make skillful sailors. But the whole experience built on a number of things I'd started to reflect on.

I was quite young when I started as a trainer. I was passionate about being a good trainer, so I hoovered up as many tips as I could from experienced trainers and books on training. They mostly offered tips on how to dress, set up exercises, stay calm in front of a group of people, and not use filler words when presenting. All the things I needed to do to be that shiny happy trainer, most of which constituted a sort of universal rules of training. I learned to get into the room the day before to arrange the tables. Manage group discussions so you didn't spend more time on the exercises than the instructional designers had allowed. And never walk in front of the projector beam, which they still say today. If you've been training for more than 15 minutes, you know what I'm talking about.

What's funny is that none of these universal rules would have helped me in that workshop in Moscow. For my first 15 years as a trainer, I worked hard to be the shiny happy trainer, from delivering learning in Sydney, Australia, to running seminars in Frankfurt; from facilitating leadership workshops in the South of France to teaching video on the U.S. West Coast. But I must confess, I have discovered that people in my classes get more when I'm not being that shiny happy trainer, when I stop giving smart presentations with cute PowerPoint slides and let them struggle with the learning. When I don't worry about how good I look in front of a group and instead focus on how well they were doing with their learning. Moscow helped me see some of this, along with thousands of people who have been in my classes over the years.

A big takeaway for me was that when we bomb as a trainer, whether it's our fault or not, people can still learn. In fact, sometimes they learn more when we bomb because we're forced to step out of the way. A question I took home from Moscow was whether we as trainers think we play a larger role in a participant's learning than we really do. Being solidly prepared and doing all the right things does not necessarily prevent training-room disasters. Being agile and focused on learners' needs is what counts.

One of my all-time favorite jobs was as a talk show host. I was in my early 20s and was on the air every morning from 6 to 8:30. My job required good presentations skills, so as I transitioned into the training world, I found myself relying on those skills to become that shiny happy trainer. Now, more than 25 years later, I wonder whether having those skills actually gets in the way of participant learning. The jury is still out for me on that, but we'll explore the idea throughout the book.

The Gritty Reality of Training

Training is not glamorous work. People will still stomp out of your class for one reason or another. They'll write nasty things on evaluations and talk about you behind your back. You'll still miss flight connections and not make it home for your kids' school play. You'll have arguments with instructional designers, managers, and learners. And your days will start early, as you beat your participants into the classroom, and end late, as you wait for the last one to leave.

When people think of the ideal trainer, they often think of the shiny happy trainer. They equate the work of training to keynote speaking: Present well and develop a good stage presence. It's an embedded idea that over the years I have started to question. A good trainer is someone who helps other people learn. They do more than just talking through PowerPoint slides.

I hope you'll join me on a journey through the gritty reality of being a trainer. Just as Christina introduced me to the real Moscow, I hope to introduce you to the real training life. If you're already living that life, I hope this book will encourage you as you do good work. There's a chance, as you read this book, that you might think I stole your stories, changed the names, and made them my own. No, I didn't. But much of what I've been through over the past 25 years or so, across

25 countries, is what many seasoned trainers experience every day around the globe.

I'm hoping that by sharing some of my stories—and those of a number of others who have been kind to add their experiences—I can assure you that you're not the only one. And for those days you think, "Gee, I didn't present well" or "My slide deck was crap," I hope you'll realize that the notion of a shiny happy trainer who's slick and well organized is simply a myth.

Some trainers are employed within organizations—some working in a talent or training department, others on their own, slogging away as their company's sole trainer. Others are freelancers who find themselves working with different people in different organizations in different cities every week. Some work in corporate, others in government agencies or for nonprofits. While the details of what we do and where we do it may be different, many of the dynamics are the same. And we face many of the same challenges: How can we help people be better at what they do, and how can we link their performance to their organization's needs?

What I share is intended for anyone who works in training and wants to balance the tension of helping both the individual and the organization. And the key to being successful in that endeavor is understanding something that's at the heart of everything we do. Learning. But what is it?

2

LEARNING TAKES PRACTICE

Being a student is easy. Learning requires actual work.
—William Crawford

WHEN I WAS A KID, I was fired by three piano teachers. Not all at once, mind you. My first teacher, Mrs. Humbleside, was a crotchety old woman about 65 years old. At just over five-feet tall, she towered over my six-year-old frame, especially when she sat me down on the piano stool for our sessions. "You must practice 10 minutes every day," she commanded.

If you have ever learned a musical instrument or tried to, you know it's hard work. What makes it worse is that piano life starts with practicing simple five-finger exercises. And they're boring. Once you have that down, you learn scales. C Major scale—the happy scale. D Minor scale—the sad one. B Minor Melodic scale—the sad and complicated one that changes halfway through. Then there are arpeggios and contrary motion scales. But when I was six, I preferred playing in the dirt with toy cars.

So I didn't practice. When I went into the room at home with the piano, I daydreamed about playing with die-cast-metal toy cars and riding my BMX bike. Three weeks later, Mrs. Humbleside sat me down on the piano stool, and I kind of knew what was coming. And she used the art of fear to try to get me practicing: "I'm a dragon, you know, so you'd better start practicing." The following week, she fired me. She later told my mother I had replied, "Do you breathe fire?" Apparently, even when I was six years old, I was precocious.

Mrs. McKinsey was much less scary. She had perpetual frown lines tattooed across her forehead and always looked serious. But she was a friend of my mother's, so she put up with me for six months before she fired me: "Jonathan really needs practice to realize his potential." So I packed my music books and was dispatched to her successor, Mrs. Primlon, a prim and proper English lady in her 60s. She was tall and thin and had wispy white hair. Mrs. Pimlon had better staying power. She lasted two and a half years before issuing my pink slip.

Despite the difficulties I presented them, these women were wise in many ways. They understood that if I were ever to learn to play piano, I had to practice. Investing their time and taking my parents' money made little sense if I didn't. As far as local teachers were concerned, they had good reputations and were respected for helping kids learn piano. But they knew that it didn't matter how good they were as teachers if I didn't practice.

If only I had known that when I started out as a trainer. Early on, I thought that the work I did designing and delivering learning was what led to success. But I have to confess that my experiences taught me what my piano teachers knew. It's the work of the learner—practice—that makes learning successful.

Practice

Recognizing that practice is at the heart of learning isn't difficult. Malcolm Gladwell wrote about this in his book *Outliers* (2011), when he referenced that it takes 10,000 hours—about 10 years at 20 hours a week—of sustained practice to be exceptional at something. But practice is often overlooked, especially when we think about high performance.

People don't learn by simply hearing or seeing something. They need to practice it. Learning takes time, energy, and focus, and it's no different in the world of adult learning than when learning to play the piano. If my piano teacher sat down and played Beethoven's "Fur Elise" to me, then let me go home without first practicing it, I'd forget it. She needed to see me practice it, so she could redirect me if I hit the wrong notes or played too loud or soft. And she needed me to practice it so I could more easily remember it when I practiced at home. Having her simply perform the piece in front of me was not enough for me to learn, just as performing a training presentation, such as talking through some slides, is not enough for employees to learn. It must include practice.

INSIDER TIP

I like theory but sometimes it helps to have real stories that show theory in action. Matthew Syed's book *Bounce* does just that. While it's written for a general audience, it shows how practice has been instrumental in the success of famous people from Mozart to David Beckham.

In my experience working with trainers around the globe, most folks agree that practice is important. But I see many pay lip service to this simple truth rather than incorporating it into their work. How? I see half-day training sessions with two and a half hours' worth of PowerPoint slides. I see learning plans for one-day workshops with

10 learning objectives, which are impossible to deliver unless they are being presented and not practiced. I've lost track of how many training sessions I've seen that are little more than a performance by the trainer, where learners listen and watch but don't engage in practice. The notion that training is a delivery of information is so entrenched that a lot of corporate training programs around the world are little more than information dumps.

Marc Wilner, a training manager at the California software company Ellie Mae, has a creative approach to delivering learning. With close to two decades in the training field, he told me what he's seen over the years when it comes to practice: "There's not enough. I've worked for multiple organizations where we dump so much content that people choke on it." I couldn't put it better. But why do we dump so much? Is it because we like talking? Is it because learners believe that they get more value when we talk more? Is it because our bosses think we need to cover more content?

If I've learned anything in my almost 30 years of training, it's that learning is less about what I do as a trainer and more about what the learner does to construct skills and knowledge. But the prevailing belief in many organizations, and sadly some training departments, is that learning happens when we deliver content. To use Wilner's words, it's about what we give learners to choke on. As a consequence, trainer education and development programs teach trainers more about presentation skills than what learners need to do to learn. And managers judge trainers' professionalism more on how smoothly a session went than on the new skill or knowledge the learners built as a result of the learning experience.

Like many people, I discovered this as part of my professional journey. Early in my life, I earned my bread and butter as a talk show host. To survive, I had to be more than just a good presenter. So as I transitioned into training, I took my skills as a presenter with me and aimed to present information in a polished and interesting way. But over time, I discovered that when I was less polished, was less in control of the classroom, and allowed more time for learners to play around and make mistakes, learning was deeper.

What was also interesting was that I always knew this. My academic background was in adult learning, and I knew that effective learning needs to be interactive. But I always fell back into the mindset of spraying people with content, albeit in a polished and entertaining way. If only I'd known what my piano teachers had known: No matter how good I was, people might still not learn a thing. Over the years, I've concluded that successful trainers break most of the rules they were taught in their two-day train-the-trainer workshops. These are the universal but unwritten rules that exist in our field that I mentioned in the introduction.

This is not a textbook on learning. But to make sense of some of the things I share later, we need to be on the same page about learning and what it is. So, before we move on to the day-to-day practical stuff of being a trainer, let's dig into a bit of learning science. Some of this is complex so bear with me—I've kept it to the essentials.

INSIDER TIP

If you're searching for an accessible book that explains in clear terms what must happen for learning to take place, grab a copy of *Make It Stick* by Peter C. Brown, Henry L. Roediger III, and Mark A. McDaniel. I like it so much it's on my list of top five books I recommend for participants in my train-the-trainer programs.

The Learning Formula

There are many theories about how learning happens, so it's possible to deconstruct the topic in different ways. I don't rate any theory higher or lower than another, but if you and I were sipping coffee at Starbucks, and you said, "Jonathan, explain in 20 seconds how learning takes place when learning to perform a task," I'd say that three things need to happen:

- The learner needs to understand the task and how it is performed.
- The learner needs to remember the task so that they can perform it in class and practice it.
- The learner needs to perform the task outside the classroom, in the real world.

I often call it the learning formula: Understanding + Memory + Application = Learning. When participants work to understand something, deploy deliberate strategies to remember it, and then apply it in the real world, learning takes place. We could get more detailed, but let's leave it at that high level for now. You'll notice that these things are what the learner does, not what the trainer does. Our role is to help the learner do them.

It's crazily simple. And yet for many years, I focused on getting the presentation right when I should have focused on ensuring that the learner was doing what was necessary to understand, remember, and apply. Sure, I gave good feedback and all the stuff that goes with practice, but I probably never went far enough. I was more concerned about using the correct colored pens on flipcharts and whether participants understood what I was saying.

That said, there's nothing wrong with good presentations and we should try to be easily understood. Horribly designed slides and muddled instructions can derail learner-centered practice. But learning is really about memory and how the participants create and use it. People make sense of the world and the tasks they perform by organizing their memories into mental models that help them do things automatically. Learning is the process of building and refining these mental models. My three music teachers understood this. They also knew it would be hard work; I demonstrated a serious lack of commitment because I preferred playing in the dirt with model cars. In fact, I was actually good at playing in the dirt simply because I did it so often. They were wise to sack me.

The cognitive process of learning is straightforward. I'll skip the jargon and use my learning formula to run through some basics. If you got into training like I did and were schooled to be a shiny happy trainer, seeing what's involved in learning will turn your trainer world upside down. I found it liberating, because it empowered me to better support learners.

Understanding

The first step in learning a task is to make sense of it. This sounds easier than it is because tasks have different layers of complexity that involve why, where, and how the task is performed, along with different ways it may be performed.

People make sense of what they learn by taking information into their brains and processing it through their existing memories. This could be information they saw, heard, touched, smelled, or tasted. As soon as they experience these things, their brain forms an immediate memory. I like to think of these memories as data, much as memory in a computer is data.

A classic example of this process in action is when a child touches a hot plate, usually after being told not to. The sensation of burning gets stored in long-term memory. The child processes this piece of data and its associated pain, creating a mental model explaining that hot plates are hot and when touched, they hurt. Over time, this mental model becomes more sophisticated, including facts such as hot plates burn skin only when they are switched on.

Anything someone experiences is processed through their existing memories, which help form these mental models. So if that child sees me place my hand near a hot plate, she might yell out to me, "Don't! You'll burn your hand." Or if she has learned that it needs to be switched off, she might cry out, "Hey, that hot plate *might* be hot." The subtle difference shows how knowledge can have different layers of complexity.

Through observing, reading, experimenting, and even playing games, people will form memories in order to learn. This might entail being told something or sitting back and reflecting on a topic, such as in a training class. But the most powerful learning happens when people discover something through trial and error or experimentation. Ironically, a lot of time is spent in the training world giving presentations, hoping people will form their understanding through what we present, when in many cases, it's the least effective method.

Remembering

Memory is fundamental to learning. And while drawing on existing memories is the first step to learning something, building new memories is what training is all about. These new memories are the mental models used to perform tasks and form concepts. The process of building memory is hard work, and helping learners do this is probably the most important task for trainers. What makes it tricky is that humans are wired to forget things.

Back in 1885, the German psychologist Hermann Ebbinghaus proposed what he called the "forgetting curve." He suggested that within days, people forget half of what they remember. The implication here is that folks sitting in training classes are more likely to forget something the trainer says than remember it. Our job as trainers is to do everything we can to help participants *not* forget things.

Participants can impede the natural process of forgetting by retrieving a memory. This can happen in many ways. A participant might talk about the memory, draw it, or perform the skill attached to the memory. It's like the old phrase says, "Use it or lose it."

If you think about training classes you've attended, you'll likely remember more about the discussions and breakout sessions than what the trainer actually said. That's because discussion involves retrieving and processing memories. Practicing a task involves retrieval, too. If I want to memorize Beethoven's "Fur Elise" on the piano, I'll remember it better by practicing it than listening to a record of someone else playing it. The more I retrieve and develop a memory, the stronger it becomes.

This has huge implications for trainers. For learners to get more out of their time in the classroom, they need to do more practice and we need to do less presentation. Are you picking up my theme here? We worry about being good presenters when we need to worry about learners being good "practicers." Yes, I made that word up, but you know what I mean.

Earlier, I referenced Malcolm Gladwell and his book *Outliers*. While he talked about 10,000 hours of practice, it's not just any practice that works. Gladwell was drawing on research by Anders Ericsson and others (1993), who later pointed out that two important points of his research didn't make it into Gladwell's book. First, 10,000 was an average. Some people need more time for practice, others less. Second, Ericsson stipulated that learners needed to employ what he calls deliberate practice.

Many people think of practice as doing something over and over. This is massed practice, and what many people did in college the night before an exam: They crammed. They read and reread the textbook, underlining important points. While they were able to remember key points during the exam, they forgot them later.

Deliberate practice, on the other hand, is a specific set of practice strategies that plays off the forgetting curve and strengthens memory by forcing us to let a memory fade but grabbing it before it totally disappears. This process is much more difficult, messy, and unpredictable for the learner. It sometimes leads to more initial mistakes, but it causes much stronger connections to memory.

Trainers can deploy a number of deliberative practice strategies. One comes directly from Ebbinghaus's research and is known as spaced learning. The trainer will ask a learner to remember a key skill several times at a high level, but make the interval between each retrieval longer. For example, if helping someone learn software, the trainer will ask the learner to remember it one day after it was taught, then again two days later, then three days later, and so on.

Interleaving is another deliberate learning strategy that involves learners switching between topics of study. Let's say I am attending a three-hour class on training basics that covers how to write a learning objective, conduct a debrief, and write a Level 1 evaluation survey. The intuitive way to design the class is to spend an hour understanding and practicing each task in succession: the first hour on objectives, the second on debriefing, and the third on evaluation. However, studies show that if we switch between these topics throughout the three hours—that is, interleave them—memory connections will be stronger. So we'd instead spend 20 minutes on objectives, 20 minutes on debriefing, and then 20 minutes on evaluation. Then in the second hour, we'd switch between them again, and again in the final hour. Each time we switch topics, our memory of the previous topic fades. When we come back to it, we have to do the hard work of retrieval before it totally fades, which strengthens connections to the memory.

There are other forms of deliberate practice, but as I said, this is a quick overview, not a textbook. What I've been fascinated by over the past 10 years is neuroscience. Studies show that when we form memories, we actually fire neurons. These neurons light up like a Christmas tree on brain scans. There are loads of implications here, but one that I think is easy to forget is that learning—understanding, remembering, and applying—is a physiological process. That's why learning new stuff is hard work. It's tiring. Not that I've been to the gym more than three times in my life, but getting people to learn is like doing weights at the gym.

Applying

The final stage of learning a new skill is applying it. Application essentially describes the raison d'être for learning and is what sets workplace learning apart from, say, school or university learning. For example, at school, people learn calculus to pass the math exam at the end of the year. Even if you were an engineering major or someone who planned to use calculus on a daily basis, you were still taught calculus so you could get an A on your test. In the workplace, people learn a skill because it helps them do their work better.

Companies generally don't fund training departments for the sake of having training departments. Commercial organizations expect that when they spend money for salespeople to take a training course, it will help them sell more products. Government agencies invest in training to offer taxpayers better services, such as efficiency and cost savings. Nonprofits invest in training to allow them to better serve society.

Just as good school teachers understand that their job is to help students perform well in exam conditions, good trainers understand that their job is to help learners do their work better, which leads to better organizational performance. So they look to better support learning beyond the classroom, when it is practiced and performed in the workplace. Delivering learning is no good if people simply leave our virtual sessions or face-to-face workshops with a memory of how to do something, but not the ability to apply that skill in the real world.

As I wrote an early draft of this chapter, I sat on the 18th deck of an ocean cruiser. High up on the ship, I watched the crew perform their safety drills in the water below. They lowered the emergency rafts into the water and tested their readiness for what everyone hopes will never happen: the boat capsizing. For the crew, learning is not about going to some nice presentation on how boats float; it's about being mentally and physically ready to perform the unthinkable. For sales trainers, it might be how to close the sale faster; for administrative workers in a local county office, it might be how to use new software; for managers, it might be how to resolve a staff conflict in a heated situation.

Successful learning is about building skills that are robust enough to use in the real world. Sure, I want the sailors to learn how to lower a life raft when the boat is moored in port, but I really want them to practice it in choppy seas so that if they ever have to use those skills, they'll know how to help someone into the life raft in realistic conditions. Application is the whole point of workplace learning, and it has many implications for trainers. We need to make sure that our learning objectives are relevant, focused, and approved by the business. Our instructional exercises must mirror real conditions. (How often have you heard participants chuckle, "Oh, this isn't how it works in the real world"?) We need to provide support for learners to deliberately practice new skills after they leave our classes.

We will talk more about the need for practice when we touch on the learning ecosystem in a later chapter. But I'm often amazed at how many training programs are designed in a vacuum, in which the learning happens in the classroom but stops when the clock runs out. Of course, the pressures within the working ecosystem have evolved to create this rhythm—the trainer is committed to deliver a two-day experience and then move on to the next commitment. They rarely have the resources to go back to learners in the workplace and help reinforce what they learned. The learners are largely on their own.

More Physical Therapist Than Keynote Speaker

The notion of a shiny happy trainer—the consummate professional who is entertaining and says all the right things—is also common outside training departments. Many organizational leaders view trainers and the work they do in the classroom similarly to how they view keynote speakers. It's just that they give a presentation in front of 20 people instead of 1,000. Trainer job descriptions often list presentation or platform skills at the top. But how often do you see them list skills associated with helping participants create understanding, construct memories, and apply skills to the workplace?

I have nothing against keynote speakers—I do a lot of keynotes myself. But keynotes have a different purpose than training events and generally function as the capstone of a conference attracting hundreds, often thousands, of people. They're usually presented by thought leaders or celebrities who share ideas to provoke, inspire, or motivate large groups of people, and they help attract people to a conference.

Training does not generally exist as part of a conference to increase attendance, but as part of an organization's budget to improve talent so that it can achieve specific business goals. It's a service very specifically designed to help people learn new knowledge and skills or deepen existing ones. Certainly, there will be times within a training program where a short presentation is appropriate. But it is a mistake to emulate keynote speaking in our work.

The trainer's work is more like physical therapy. When you visit the physical therapist, you don't sit there and listen to them talk about how muscles need stretching. They stretch your muscles. It hurts and it's hard work, but that's how you heal. And they don't just leave it at that. They know that unless you keep stretching every day between that appointment and the next, your healing will be slow. So, they show you the exercise and have you demonstrate that you know how to do it. And they expect you to do it at home.

Just as stretching your muscles in the physical therapist's office after a sports accident is hard, painful work, real learning is hard work, too.

INSIDER TIP

Looking for a book that looks at both the art and science of learning but in the context of corporate training? Elaine Biech's bestselling book *The Art and Science of Training* does just that. It's another book that's made my top five list for folks attending my train-the-trainer workshops.

Implications

While that's a lot of theory to process, it represents the heart of what we as learning professionals do. So, what does it mean for how we do it?

Well, trainers who want results will craft learning experiences that engage learners in activities that help them discover the learning and retain it through practice. They will be comfortable with asking questions rather than always offering an answer, knowing learners have the resources to almost always find those answers. They will plan lots of practice to ensure the skills are developed and remembered. They will avoid the typical presentation in favor of activities such as class experiments, discussions, and instructional games. It's all about retrieval—learners need to play with the content, wrestle with it, try it.

Mrs. Humbleside got this. I had to practice. If I didn't, I wouldn't learn to play the piano, no matter how much "presenting" she did during our sessions. I bet she'd have been a great corporate trainer. Our job isn't to present. It's to get participants to do the work of building and practicing their learning.

A Trainer Reacts to Facilitation Adversity

Lou Russell

I HAVE ALWAYS CONSIDERED facilitating learning a sacred calling, and I like to call myself a facilitator because it's so critical that we facilitate and not just train or tell. That doesn't mean all will go smoothly. We are just people, with good and bad days, easy and hard travel, happy and angry learners. And yet, the show must go on and learning must occur, as demonstrated in three experiences from my past.

The group at the 1995 ASTD International Conference & EXPO in Indianapolis was engaged, my delivery flowing, and the microphone clipped to me was working. Then, I noticed something white on the floor and shouted into my mic, "What is this? OMG, it's someone's underwear!" I quickly kicked the underwear under a table and continued, while the conference room monitor carefully retrieved them.

This is something I shouldn't have said, but no one seemed to mind, and we continued to completion. Clearly, screaming "OMG" in the middle of a conference session and discussing underwear is not good facilitator behavior. But surprisingly, I still ended up getting good reviews and learning occurred for the participants. I'll always wonder how women's underwear appeared in the middle of the floor. For what it's worth, I'm going with static cling in reused pants.

More recently, I taught project management to a large group of engineers. A very angry supervisor entered the room last, sulking into a back chair. With everyone now in attendance, I facilitated a walk around exercise to make new teams. He found five other angry people to sit with him. I thought to myself, "What a jerk!" He continued to glare and not participate. After a quick break, I had a miraculous thought. Something horrible must have happened to him before he came to class. This empathetic mindset changed everything—I behaved differently toward him, and he responded. We never know what's going on in anyone else's life, and it's important to remember training is not about you, the facilitator; instead, it's about the participants and their learning. I later heard that his boss demanded he go at the last minute even though he was the expert in the topic.

Lastly, I once taught for one of our training partners at U.S. Central Command. When I arrived, I was surprised to find that no electronics were allowed in the building (including my laptop with the course slides), cell phones weren't permitted either (couldn't dial for help), and some of my materials had been destroyed because of security. I was accompanied everywhere. I managed my EQ, or emotional intelligence, determined to make it work. It was a great group of people, and the class went well. Looking back, I noted that I had not talked to the coordinator prior to the workshop, having assumed that someone else had (a totally normal process). However, I now never forget the adage, "Don't assume—it makes an ASS out of U and ME."

How you react to adversity determines your success as a facilitator. Notice and choose.

Lou Russell is the managing practice director of Moser Consulting and author of seven books for trainers, which range from IT leadership to project management.

3

I DON'T TRY TO BE A GOOD PRESENTER ANYMORE

Anything worth doing well is worth doing poorly at first.
—Roy Langdon

MARYLEBONE HIGH STREET used to be one of those shabby London streets with shops that were shuttered on the weekend, except for those dark little ones selling radios and electric razors. Today it's one of the most fashionable streets in London, lined with high-end shops and restaurants and home to loads of cultural heritage. I'm fond of Marylebone, not because I'm a fashionable socialite, but because this old London street was once the center of my world.

I had a desk in the BBC building on Marylebone High Street, just near Paddington Street. For a good part of that time, my wife and I lived a few blocks away, in a two-story flat on the corner of Wimpole and New Cavendish Streets. Decades before that, Paul McCartney had lived in the flat across the road—it's where he wrote the song "Yesterday." We were just down from where Professor Higgins, from the musical *My Fair Lady,* lived and educated Eliza Doolittle. And McCartney wasn't the only performer who has lived in Marylebone over the years. Madonna called herself a resident, as did a range of other British performers.

The district was a great place to live; it had both classy and mid-range restaurants, an artisan cheese shop, and a Waitrose supermarket. It was within walking distance of all the things that were important to me: Regent's Park; the shops on Oxford Street, such as Selfridges and John Lewis; our church; and of course my BBC office. I loved the cultural heritage of Marylebone and the fact it had been home to so many performers over the years. Because in a funny sort of way, I felt like a performer myself. Not a stage or screen performer, mind you; it was on a much smaller scale. I held forth as a shiny happy trainer in front of workshop participants in Training Room 3, on the second floor of 35 Marylebone High Street.

Enter From Stage Left, Jonathan the Trainer-Performer

While training is about helping people learn new skills, many also see performance as an important element of a trainer's work. That's why many trainer job descriptions list presentation skills as a requirement. Performance terms such as *audience, stage, props, script,* and *limelight* litter the training lexicon. And don't ask how many times someone has told me, "If you're good onstage, you'll make a good trainer." Well, that naturally suited me. I did well in school plays years before, appeared on a TV show or two as a teenager, and in my 20s was a talk show host on a two-bit radio station. So I was set for prime time in Marylebone High

Street in my own small, special way. While I was educating folks in writing, digital storytelling, and creativity workshops, I also saw myself as performing.

Every morning, I set up my workshops much like I set up my talk show. I prepared what I'd say and made sure it was aligned with my PowerPoint slides. I mapped out the stories I'd present that would help explain tough concepts. I planned everything down to the minute. I practiced words that were hard to pronounce, memorized technical jargon, and even crafted questions I would ask in advance. To ensure that I had the credibility of an expert trainer, I dressed "a level above the learner" because a colleague had told me that was the professional way, whatever that meant. I monitored my body language to make sure that it was open and smooth, and that I didn't pace the room too much, walk in front of the projector beam, have my back to the class, or fall into some sort of nervous twitch. Ninety minutes before class, I'd arrange the tables to ensure the optimum learning experience, check that the equipment worked, and play music to set the tone as people walked in. I artfully followed that universal set of unwritten training rules everyone seems to know; I was the epitome of the shiny happy trainer who delivered what I considered to be, and many still do today, the polished workshop experience. It got me mostly great Level 1 evaluation scores. I averaged in the threes and fours.

Yet despite my commitment to performing well in front of the class, I was a member of the learner-centered crowd. I was fresh out of graduate school, with bachelor's and master's degrees in adult education. I was influenced by the work of Carl Rogers and Malcolm Knowles, among others. And I'd written many times that learning takes place for the learner through practice and told it to anyone who listened. (Just ask anyone I worked with at the BBC—I could quote every learning theory under the sun.)

But in reality, my commitment was academic, because much of my practice was burdened by the need to put on a good show. Oh, I didn't call it a good show. Rather than create a safe and messy space for learners to forge their learning through nonlinear practice and trial and error, I delivered content in a slick and polished way. I said things like "There are no wrong answers" because well, that's what you said, right? It is from this kind of polished presentation that many people judge a trainers' competency—whether it be in evaluation sheets after a workshop or a manager dropping in to observe you in the classroom. Did the trainer do and say the right things? And while I planned multiple exercises for participants to do the work of practice, I have to confess I was probably more interested in my performance. But it paid off; I got good evaluation scores.

Of course, there's nothing wrong with polished presentations when they help people learn. But when polishing the presentation becomes more important than creating a space for the learner to learn, the learners lose out, as we discussed in chapter 2. What's worse, it's very easy to think we're providing that space when much still revolves around what happens at the front of the classroom. Presentation-style training is pervasive, for all sorts of reasons. Maybe it's ego—isn't it nice to have people sit there and listen to you, even if deep down you know it's because their boss ordered them to attend? Some organizations even have a culture that expects training to be about presentations. And sometimes I think rating a trainer on their presentations skills—something that's quick and simple to do—is easier than rating them, or the program, using Level 2, 3, or 4 evaluation data. So in organizations around the world, trainers who value practice-based learning are pulled toward delivering good presentations and away from crafting opportunities for people to learn.

All this is not helped by topics discussed at training conferences. One conference in Europe had the following sessions: "How to Wow Your Audience," "Stage Presence for Trainers," and "Opera Singer Teaches Vocal Techniques for Trainers." Not that we can't learn from these, but they distract from our real work.

If I'm being honest, I constantly found myself sucked into this vortex. I'd hear colleagues being praised for giving good presentations, and worry about what people thought of *my* presentations. I kept asking myself, *Was I confident? Erudite? Polished?* I was terrified someone would say, "He was boring." Or, "He used filler words four times in one minute." Or, "He had to look at his notes to remember a key term." It was a huge pressure, especially given that as we present, learners have nothing to do but watch and critique our performance. At least, when they're not checking their email.

A few years ago in a Midwest steakhouse, I had an epiphany that liberated me from this stress. It came to me that focusing on being a good presenter can be a big, fat waste of time. And it causes too much stress: We set ourselves up to fail. Who cares if my back is to the class for a few seconds while I scrawl an important point on the whiteboard? Does that really compromise learning? But attend any one of the many train-the-trainer programs around the world, and you'll see new trainers being chastised by other new trainers for doing just that. Or for using too many filler words. Or for not taking control of the stage. Why do we waste so much time expecting trainers to be slick presenters if learning really happens when we give learners the chance to discuss, argue, struggle, experiment, build, role-play, and engage in other forms of deliberate practice?

If you think I'm being critical of many trainers, bear in mind that this is directed as much at me as anyone. While I was helping learners engage in practice activities back in my Marylebone days, I was secretly worried about my presentations. Part of it was ego, another part immaturity, and another part insecurity. These are the worries that trainers I coach around the globe tell me are very real for them, too. The performance mindset is a dangerous influence in the training world, even when most of us say that we're committed to a learner-centered practice. It detracts from helping learners build their learning.

LANGUAGE MATTERS

The training world is full of words and assumptions from the entertainment world. Take, for example, the word *audience*, commonly used to refer to learners. The people in our classrooms are not members of an audience or a set of adoring fans. (In fact, more often than not, many participants don't even want to be there.) If we use this term, it's easy to fall into the performance mode and "play to the audience."

Another word from the language of performance is *energy*. How often have you heard the phrase, "He brings energy into the room"? It conjures up images of the shiny happy trainer bouncing around the room. Isn't that what a street performer does, or an entertainer in Vegas? Our job is to get learners doing the work of learning—they're the ones who should be bouncing around the room and engaging with other learners. They're the ones who should be firing their neurons. We need to be helping them find that energy to engage in deeper learning.

Other terms have crept into our world that deserve critiquing, too, such as *knowledge transfer*. I've used this phrase forever, but is the transfer of knowledge really possible? People build their knowledge based on new memories seen through existing ones. It's not as if learners copy and paste knowledge from a USB stick—well, not yet, anyway. And how about the word *delivery*? Do we really "deliver" learning?

These words and more end up muddying the true responsibility of the trainer.

Epiphany in the Cornhusker State

It took a stint in Lincoln, Nebraska, a long way from Marylebone High Street, to truly learn that I didn't need to be a good presenter. Lincoln is one of those Midwest towns where everything is just right. It has one of my favorite steak restaurants, Misty's Steakhouse, and in 2013 it was rated America's Happiest and Healthiest City to Live In by *Business Insider* (Zeveloff 2013). The people are friendly—not high-strung, like some of us who live in the Washington, D.C., area.

I delivered my first-ever video boot camp for trainers in Lincoln, so I have extra affection for this town. The local community college and ATD chapter announced the boot camp and it sold out within days, so we scheduled a second for the day after, which also filled up. The boot camp is a really cool program—in one day, it teaches trainers the A to Z of making short instructional videos with their smartphone. Back then, when I did it in Lincoln, we used flip cameras rather than phones. We started early and finished late because there was so much content to cover. Every minute was carefully planned to cover the salient points: learning and editorial theory, how to shoot on a flip camera, and how to edit. (Notice how I was thinking about delivering content, not helping learners discover or build new skills?)

To get through everything, I had to be strict with time and deliver a finely tuned presentation. If it wasn't polished, people would lose interest, or so I'd been told by mentors over the years. If it wasn't clear and well constructed, learners would get lost. Instructions were important, too—they had to be super clear. If you've ever taught software, whether it was an accounting system or Excel, you'll know what I'm talking about. There's a lot going on, and it's easy for participants to become confused. Add to that the fact that a third of the class will jump ahead to experiment even when you plead for them to wait, and another third will lag so far behind that you need a TARDIS to go back and fetch them. (In my experience, you generally only have about a third of participants with you at the point of instruction.) Then you need to factor in the different skill levels of the learners. In one class, I actually had a participant raise his hand and ask what a mouse was. I'm not kidding.

As a shiny happy trainer, I planned everything meticulously, especially the software training. I had slide decks, props, and notes. I spent extra time breaking down the editing process and software commands to take learners through the steps. (That presentation was planned for 45 minutes.) It was just like the old days on Marylebone High Street. And everything ended up going well, half because the college and ATD folks were so wonderful on logistics. At the end of the day, everyone adjourned to the college theater to watch the videos people had made—as if we were at a professional screening—and the college provided popcorn. Except for two or three people who didn't finish, everyone made really cool instructional videos. But the fact some didn't make it through really bugged me. And like most shiny happy trainers, I blamed myself. What had I done wrong to prevent these folks from finishing their video?

That night at Misty's Steakhouse, pairing a prime rib with a pint of citrus wheat beer, I tried to figure out what in my presentation had blocked their learning. Was it the process? I had designed it following ADDIE, conducting a thorough task analysis. Surely my presentation was clear enough. A number of folks had even told me it was one of the clearest software demos they'd seen. That was good for my ego. But then it dawned on me: While I was obsessed by my performance, I'd forgotten some important things from cognitive psychology—the stuff I was enamored with in college.

My task analysis was based on how I thought about the software and workflow, not how the learners would. I was drawing from my mental models, and while many of the participants could relate, others simply couldn't match mine with theirs. Furthermore, I was restricting their progress by insisting they follow my demo, when some tasks could be completed several ways. For example, if you need to bold a word or letter in Microsoft Word, you can select it and hit Control + B. You can also do it by going to the ribbon tab and selecting Bold. Does it really matter which way someone does it when both get the same result? As a shiny happy trainer, I had presented the steps as if they were the only correct way. If someone is used to doing a task another way, should I force them to do it my way? I realized I needed to change something. What I did—just a small thing—taught me a profound lesson.

Sitting there in Misty's, I decided to do a free-for-all the following day. So for the second boot camp, when we got to the topic of editing, I said, "I'm not going to bore you with a step-by-step guide to editing." It felt weird to say this, as if I were breaking one of those universal training rules. "I'll show you some editing at a high level, real quick," I said. "Then you can play with it. As you're playing, I'll wander around and be your coach." I demonstrated how to cut together five shots and add music; it took about 15 minutes, a third of my original presentation time. Then participants started experimenting, and the room positively buzzed. The energy was no longer concentrated around me, the presenter. It was in the center of the room, with the learners. I'd stepped out of the way so they could learn.

But here's what was really exciting: Everyone finished the editing. And the standard of editing was much better than the day before. Why? Because I shut up, stopped worrying about giving the perfect presentation, and created the space for learners to build their own learning. And here's something else: Rather than trust myself to get my presentation right, I trusted the learners to use their resources to learn. Quite the epiphany.

Step Back to Allow Learners to Breathe—and Learn

I know it's possible that I'm just lousy at explaining content, so shutting up and stepping out of the way was best for the learners. But I can't help wonder if too many of us make it harder for learners by being slaves to our presentation plans and content. We force learners to make sense of their learning using our mental models, experiences, and language, rather than their own more accessible mental models. Or we force them to use an instructional designer's mental model, which trainers don't always fully understand. And we rob participants of an opportunity to make a powerful, emotional connection to the learning.

And speaking of emotional connections, there's another good reason to create space for learners to play with content. It's called dopamine, and it works when we help learners discover answers on their own. If we give the learner a problem to solve and they solve it, they get a sense of elation and the brain releases dopamine, often called the pleasure chemical. Dopamine is linked to a lot of things, but the one that interests us is memory formation. If we can create an opportunity in which the learner has to solve a problem and is able to solve it, the dopamine boosts the work of deliberate practice to ensure better retention.

I've experienced this firsthand. I've taken to making furniture in my spare time. My dad taught me a few carpentry tricks, and I was able to get started making simple things like shelves. But now I'm aiming for more sophisticated projects and teaching myself new techniques by reading blogs, watching YouTube videos, and experimenting. Experimenting means I make a lot of mistakes, but then I do it again correctly. Every time I master a new technique, whether it's how to stain a piece of wood or cut a miter joint, I get a buzz of satisfaction and find myself remembering it and doing the next one better. Doing something poorly at first actually offers the opportunity to perfect a skill.

You can apply discovery learning in many ways in the classroom. For example, when a learner asks a question such as "How do I adjust the volume on a video track in this software?" most trainers feel duty-bound to give the answer. Maybe we feel good being the expert or worry that we'll lose credibility if we don't have the answer. Instead, how about responding with another question: "Which menu do you think volume control would be under?" If they can't figure it out, ask another question containing a hint.

In chapter 2, I reviewed the three things that need to happen in workplace learning. People need to understand, then remember, and last, apply. It makes sense that practicing helps people remember. But not providing the answer when a participant asks a question? Don't we have to tell people the answer for them to build their understanding (the first step in the learning formula)? Many think we do and that's why so much training is based on giving presentations. But often, it's more effective not to tell them, and instead give them resources to discover and explore their way to build that learning. It's scary when you start out because you need to trust the learner and be agile to provide varying learning resources.

INSIDER TIP

When I'm busy, my creativity sometimes dries up and it takes longer to devise ways to make a session more engaging and interactive. If you can relate, save some time and grab Elaine Biech's *101 More Ways to Make Training Active*. It's packed with ways to get learners doing the work of building learning.

I Avoid Slick Training Presentations

Back when being a shiny happy trainer was important to me, being a good presenter took up a lot of my bandwidth. I still delivered valuable learning to my clients and organization, as do many people who are inadvertently pulled into the performer mindset. I know that—I see evaluations and people get results. But just imagine how we could transform corporate learning if we stopped trying to be perfect presenters and focused on helping learners be perfect practicers? What would happen if we stepped out of the way of learning?

I think it would be awesome, because we'd really show organizations why they need to rely on the talent profession through results. And while this change in focus is not an excuse to be a sloppy communicator, it would relieve us of significant pressure. Helping learners practice needs to be our first priority if we want to truly offer transformative learning.

My workshops today are nothing like my Marylebone ones. And my evaluations now average in the mid 4s and 5s because I step out of the way and trust the learners to do the learning. There are certainly times when presentations are appropriate. Topics such as aircraft maintenance or heart surgery are too dangerous to leave to discovery learning, although once the topics have been understood, practice is necessary for retention.

As much as I still love Marylebone and all its memories—the restaurants and pubs, my office, my old church, my old flat—it's probably best that I no longer live there with all the real performers. Because I'm not a performer anymore; I'm a facilitator. After all, I'm not paid to perfect my performance. My bread and butter, and that of all trainers, is earned by helping learners perfect *their* performance—something an accountant made abundantly clear to me during a phone call 15 years ago.

4

IT'S EASY TO FORGET WHY THEY HIRED US

As I tell folks, the only reason we exist—make no mistake—is our clients.
—Ginni Rometty

"You've got 50 full-time staff," the accountant began, "and 200 contract trainers." We were talking on the phone, and I could hear him turn over a piece of paper—probably an Excel spreadsheet.

He was pleasant enough, although we'd never truly seen eye-to-eye because I had refused to implement his proposal of timesheets for staff in my department. He wanted to measure trainers' input in terms of how many hours they stood in the classroom. But I thought timesheets would present an incomplete picture, because the results of a trainer's input extends beyond the time they're in a classroom. *Bean counters,* I thought. *They're all the same.*

"I was also looking at your deployment statistics," he continued. "Measured over the year, it seems your trainers are busier in the autumn than in summer." His comment was another example of the blissful ignorance people have of what trainers do. Do trainers work only when they're in the classroom? They don't do preparation? They don't consult with internal clients? They don't design new classes? Update participant guides? Offer follow-up coaching for participants in classes?

Unfortunately, the spreadsheet was not lying. But it told only part of the truth. You see, my trainers did teach more classes in the autumn and winter months because at a media company, most of the production crewmembers who attended our classes were out shooting TV shows in the summer, when the weather is best for filming. So fewer people came to workshops, especially in August, when Europe goes on summer vacation. My team thus scheduled fewer classes, which opened up a few extra weeks to do the unseen stuff of training, such as checking equipment, planning winter schedules, and conducting needs analyses our trainers didn't have time for in the winter.

"It suggests that we should be looking at an elastic workforce for your department." Notice his use of the word *it*. Not "I think we should . . ." Very clever. He deftly made it sound as if it were a third-person opinion, and he was merely the messenger. But it was his opinion, all right. Plus, he introduced me to a new buzzword: *elastic workforce,* like *rightsizing* and *downsizing*. What did he mean by that?

He laid it on the table: "We should outsource all your trainers. Only pay them when they're in the classroom." Doesn't the world look simpler when displayed on an Excel spreadsheet? Unfortunately, that simplicity is what financial managers and executives all over the world see when they make their decisions.

Trainers in many organizations are an endangered species, especially when a recession looms on the horizon. They're seen as a cost rather than an investment. When the good times dry up, the accountants say things like, "Can't we outsource?" or "What about on-the-job training?" And it's not just internal trainers who are at risk. If you're a vendor, you're also on the line when times are tight. Unless, of course, the organization understands your value.

Understanding your value means seeing a link between the cost to hire you and the return on that investment. Much of my work over the past few years has been with learning executives across North America; almost all of them have told me it's a constant struggle to help organizations see the value in trainers and talent development professionals. And it comes down to that link—ensuring trainers get it and the organizations they serve see it.

The Raison D'être for the Training Department

A few years ago, I crashed a cocktail party at an ATD conference and found myself in a huddle of trainers talking about their passion for what they do and why they'd become trainers. A guy in his mid-40s said that he'd worked as a salesman for 20 years and wanted to give back. A woman with a Texas accent said that she became a trainer because she loves seeing a light bulb go on in people's heads when they learn something new. A gentleman from New York said that he had a flair for acting, and being a trainer met his needs to be onstage.

As a former journalist, I often find myself adopting the role of provocateur. So I asked them, "What do you think motivates our employers and clients to want us to be trainers?"

The New Yorker suggested that his organization wanted a dynamic presenter to keep the audience's interest. There was that word, *audience.* The 40-something fellow said that his company wanted his breadth of experience. Only the Texan, in my mind, got close to why most organizations hire a trainer. "They like the way I help people learn," she said.

I think it starts with helping people learn, but it goes deeper than that. CEOs don't care if you're an entertaining person. They want results first and foremost, and they hire trainers and training departments to deliver results. For a retail organization, the results might be an increase in sales. For a manufacturing company, a reduction of safety accidents. For a government agency, efficiency increases. For a nonprofit, a social value. They want a team of professionals who can help staff optimize their performance.

To many trainers I meet, this is far from obvious. They see their role with them, rather than the organization, in the center. That's why some think they were hired: because they have wisdom to share. Sure, the wisdom trainers bring is important, but our ability to help people in the organization do their work better is why we were hired.

However, simply knowing that we exist to help other people do better is not enough. It's too vague. We need to be much more specific. For example, it's good to know that Acme Widgets wants to make more widgets next year. But it's better to know that Acme wants to double the production of 200 widgets per hour to 400 widgets per hour. And it's even better to know how the organization intends to do this—perhaps by installing new equipment or adopting a different workflow—as well as the timeframe for this increase, who wants it, and what's in it for the workers. Maybe it's not a factory environment. Perhaps Acme Widgets is suffering from high staff turnover, which is costing too much in terms of recruitment and tacit knowledge walking out the door. Knowing what's causing this turnover and how to fix it becomes critical.

INSIDER TIP

I hear a lot of folks talk about alignment but skip how to actually *do* it in our fast-changing world. Enter Jack and Patti Phillips. They address 12 major challenges that today's organizations face, to help talent development professionals truly connect to business needs, in their book *High Impact Capital Strategy*.

It's Easy to Be Distracted

Focusing on the business goals isn't easy because there are so many distractions, and we find ourselves balancing many tensions as we deliver learning. But if we're to demonstrate our value to the organizations we serve, we need to be sure that every learning objective is linked to a business goal that is aligned to the company's objectives and values. I've learned from bitter experience that when I talk about offering a good learning experience, managers' eyes glaze over. I can quote the latest buzzwords in our profession and tell them that we are doing things like offering microlearning content or deepening our links to the learning ecosystem, and they hardly blink. But when I tell them how I'm going to help solve a problem and am clear about how I'll do it, they become animated and buy into the process.

But even when we keep this focus, there are things that can easily throw us off. I see them as tensions that trainers and training managers have to balance for our clients if we're employed in a training department or if we're providing services as a vendor.

We Often Try to Do Too Much

A camera trainer lamented to me once that a four-week camera course had been cut to two weeks: "How can people be good camera operators if they don't know every function in the camera?" He talked about lighting. "If you're going to learn camera functions, shouldn't you learn how to shoot in low light as well as in high lighting conditions?" he asked. "Some of these folks may be sent to Baghdad and need special filters." It makes sense until you consider that these staff members were to be based in London, where the clouds hang around your shoulders. They didn't need skills for high-level lighting, which they'd forget without immediate practice. It made more sense to teach them camera features they would use day-to-day, rather than everything one needs to know about a camera, most of which they'd only very rarely use. Focusing on the immediate business need meant a class that took half the time and cost half as much. But when you're passionate about what you teach, it's easy to want to cover more than we really need.

Perhaps it's not our passion for a set of skills that distracts us from the business need, but it's our interest in a topic area. For example, a manager approaches a soft skills trainer because she's seeing conflict issues between her direct reports. They have missed deadlines because they are not working together constructively. She is convinced that they have no idea of the impact their differences and rigid behavior are having on one another or their team's productivity. "It's emotional intelligence," she tells the trainer.

Many trainers are tuned in to emotional intelligence and are super warm, human-centered people. That's why they're drawn to this work—they want to help people. Say, as an avid fan of Daniel Goleman's work, this trainer picks up on the emotional intelligence phrase and says, "You bet; we've got a two-day program for that." He then proceeds to offer a program that covers social awareness, self-awareness, and self-regulation. He's excited because he knows how powerful this program will be. Except that the manager suggested that the problem is self-awareness. Social awareness and self-regulation are not immediately relevant to the business need.

Our tendency can be to offer everything because we want to provide the complete topic. The cost-efficient solution in this case is some form of development around only self-awareness. Our job is not to offer a program; it's to help our clients solve their problems. It's easy to go beyond what the organization pays us to do.

Who Is Our True Client?

In most situations, trainers have two clients: the person who writes the check and the learner. For example, Jen runs the sales team. She hasn't hired a trainer to deliver a training class but to transform her team's success levels; she wants them to close more lucrative deals. Javier, on the other hand, works for Jen and is one of the people whom she wants to sell more. He is your client in the classroom, and the person you'll spend most time with.

What happens when Javier's perceived needs differ from Jen's? It's not an uncommon scenario where the two clash; have you ever introduced a new topic during a workshop when one or more participants resist? Sometimes their resistance is aggressive, but not always. Nevertheless, it's resistance. It often manifests along these lines: Javier says, "You really don't need to spend any time on that part of tracking customer interactions in the CRM; we've got that down pat." But you know from your conversation with Jen that this is one area she wants them to improve in, because sales have been lost when one salesperson is on vacation and no one can pick up an inquiry that is the accumulation of a series of conversations. As a trainer, you're at a crossroads because to be learner-centered, you need to listen to Javier. But, Jen hired you to help improve the team's performance, and this is a key area she said needs to be developed to ensure sales leads aren't lost when someone goes on vacation. The decision comes to deciding to whom do you serve? Can you realistically serve both?

Finding the balance between meeting both clients' needs is a critical skill and causes all sorts of internal tensions. As the saying goes, you can't serve two masters because from time to time, their needs will conflict. If you've been a trainer, your instinct may be to follow Javier because you and he have developed a constructive relationship within the context of the classroom. I have struggled with this dynamic often, such as when training journalists in workflows that I thought were inefficient but were mandated by the client. My instinct is to follow the money—in this case, Jen is the primary client and set the learning objectives to help her team achieve its business objectives. She holds the purse strings. Add to that the fact that people are often unaware of their development needs, and it takes an external perspective, like Jen's, to identify them. But once we're in the classroom, Javier is our client, because his objectives are the business goals that Jen set, and we need to help him achieve them.

I can't help but think that it starts by being clear about the learning objectives that simply define the tasks that participants should be able to perform at the end of training. Delivering learning to meet that objective is serving Jen, the client who writes the check. (By the way, I'm not talking about SMART objectives but ones that follow the established grammar of learning objectives that most in our profession follow, namely Robert Mager's action, condition, and standard formula.) Where we achieve balance with Javier as the client is that we personalize the learning experience and methods we use to help him achieve those agreed objectives.

Salesperson or Trainer?

Most trainers are proud of what they do—in fact, many see their work as a calling. Just as a journalist feels called to uncover the truth, or a nurse feels called to serve the sick, many trainers believe their purpose is to help people live their life or do their work better. But this calling can create a tension. In the media world, this tension often exists between journalists and the folks in sales and marketing. Journalists do not want the integrity of their stories compromised by sales. For example, if they're reporting on a multinational, they would be horrified if the editor told them to cut the story because the multinational bought extra advertising. A former colleague describes this barrier between sales and newsgathering as the Berlin Wall. The barrier is not as dramatic in the learning profession, but you'll often find tension when trainers who see themselves as helpers are called to sell training. But increasingly, we need to help people understand the value of real training. Perhaps *selling* is too strong a word and *being an ambassador* is a better term.

Marryam Chaudhry is the training manager at Prince William County Services Authority, in Virginia. She's worked both as an internal training manager and an executive at a training organization that provides training. She believes the role of trainers is to communicate value before, during, and after training.

"It's about learning their business needs and communicating in their language how the learning solution will help them achieve it," she told me. In a way, the trainer has to be a salesperson, which is not a comfortable role for all trainers. "Unless training clients know you're helping them and you give them updates, they will not understand the value that training brings an organization," she said.

"By learning their needs and articulating them, it keeps training focused on what the client wants, not what the trainer wants," she continued, alluding to the tension between subject matter expertise and supporting the role.

The organization pays us to do our work. And as such, we need to know what their needs are, make sure the methods we use are aligned to meet those needs, and consistently communicate our value to them. However, does that mean we should blindly follow their instructions?

The Customer Isn't Always Right

Like many trainers, I spend more time in airplanes and airports than I'd like. Any chance to drive to work rather than fly gets my attention, fast. So, when the HR director for a technology company in Reston,

Virginia, called, my ears perked up. I had my key in the ignition before she'd even half told me what she needed. Reston was a 30-minute drive from where I lived at the time. So, with a notebook and pen, dressed in a suit and tie, I was ushered into a conference room with her the following week.

"We have about 700 staff and 200 managers," she started. "And we've found that the staff have not been accountable to their managers. We think training can address this."

My first thought was, *Wow, this is interesting.* Well, to be honest, that was my second thought. My first thought, after some fast mental calculations, was, *Two hundred managers . . . groups of 15 . . . about 14 workshops. That could be work for a few months. And each night, I'd get to go home for supper, rather than be stuck in a hotel a thousand miles from home. All the while, I'd get to influence a large group of learners.*

Already intrigued, I asked, "Is accountability an issue your managers have discussed, or is it a concept they need to learn?" She looked at me strangely. "We're not talking about the managers," she said. I must have looked confused. "It's the staff—we want you to teach the staff how to be more accountable."

Perhaps I wasn't up to speed with the latest literature, but I was unaware of any study that supports the idea of training staff to be accountable. Accountability is a management issue. Managers need to either understand what accountability is or learn techniques to keep staff accountable. The HR director strongly disagreed and insisted that she'd like workshops rolled out to all staff. It was tempting for about 30 seconds—sure, I could teach a class, even if it didn't get results, and take home some good money. But as I got over that initial survival thinking, I simply couldn't justify taking this work on. Training staff in accountability wouldn't fix her company's problem; it would only fill my pockets. And as opposed to Jen's case, where training could fix her sales team's skills gap, this would not. I had little option but to decline the work; it would be unethical for me to charge money for something I couldn't do.

You may be wondering what I'm getting at here because earlier I said we need to serve the client, the implicit suggestion being that they're always right. But the customer is often wrong. Maybe it's the skill they want trained, like how to be accountable. Or they impose a pedagogical method on you—"I want you to present some PowerPoint slides on how to resolve conflict"—when you think some experiential role plays will be more powerful. (Which of course they will!) Or the manager says, "You know that three-day program on leadership—can you condense it to one day?"

Too often, trainers are asked to take on work when training is not the answer, or do training in a way that as professionals they know will not achieve the client's business needs. They know it does not represent a good investment of the client's money and time. But there is pressure to deliver it—say, your boss tells you that it could lead to a bigger contract. Or pressure exists outside the organization to show that something is being done to deal with a political crisis. For example, training is mandated in response to regulatory failures or ethics breaches. This is very common; as I write, it is happening at the FBI in response to text messages sent between two senior staffers. Training won't fix this; it's a leadership issue. But thousands of staff members who do act professionally will be forced to go through a training program that very possibly addresses a need they don't have. Think of the cost of delivering the learning and taking agents away from their desks or work in the field. I've seen this scenario play out at multiple organizations, including the BBC when I worked there. No wonder people are skeptical of training or roll their eyes when told they have to attend it.

When you're a contract trainer, it's easier to opt out of work when you think you can't effect change. Well, most of the time—we do need our income. If you're worried you'll disappoint the client because they need a trainer, don't worry. Someone else will take the work; I heard a trainer from New Mexico took the accountability contract in Reston, and I guarantee she won't be rehired because she'll be hard-pressed to show results. The unfortunate side effect is it will make the HR director more skeptical about the value of training when she realizes nothing much changed. When you turn work away respectfully, you'll be respected because you're not seen as someone who just wants the money. And your client will see that you're interested in them getting results. If they don't respect you for this, they're probably not a client you want to work for.

If you work in an organization, it's not as easy to say no to a potential client. You don't want to be insubordinate, but you don't want to be judged for work that you know will fail and could reflect on your professionalism. It's incumbent on you to have a conversation and be respectfully clear that you don't think it will work.

Back in Reston, I was asked to provide training that wouldn't work. A number of other dynamics made it impossible for me to link learning objectives to behavioral change. But we're often asked to do other things that just won't work, like employ learning methodologies inappropriately. One client at a premium-car manufacturer took issue with me because I didn't draw pictures on flipchart paper and place them on the walls during a workshop. She thought learning happened on the wall, evidently, not in learners' heads, where learners need to struggle with and process information.

Another client wanted me to incorporate learning styles into a class on instructional design. I asked, honestly, "Did you know that learning styles have been discredited by numerous studies? Designing this class based on learning styles just won't make a difference in learning reten-tion. Deliberate practice is more important." She reluctantly agreed and watched me facilitate with what I felt was significant discomfort. I used very little PowerPoint and asked learners to make a lot of decisions on how to structure the experience. Such a nonlinear approach centered on how the learner finds information, rather than how we impose it on the learner, can look messy to folks who like to fit everything neatly in a box or follow a rigidly prescribed timeline. But the client called a few weeks later and told me that her staff had radically changed their approach, and that her clients were raving about results.

I find that some clients are clueless about adult learning, or if they do have some basics, they know just enough to have a perspective that's not productive. Some think training staff is like copying a file from a USB stick and pasting it into the prefrontal cortex. This is where we need to be very clear about what we offer. Clients are experts in their business, and we need to defer to them as they describe what people should be able to do at the end of a class. But trainers need to be experts in how to help people do the work of learning.

The Rubber Hits the Road

It can be easy, in the hustle and bustle of everyday work, to forget that trainers are hired to help organizations change and meet business objectives. Just as an electrician is hired to replace a light switch or a dentist to pull a wisdom tooth, trainers are employed to help staff in an organization perform new tasks or do existing tasks better to improve the business, regardless of whether they're internal or external. How they do it varies from challenge to challenge, organization to organiza-tion, and trainer to trainer. As such, trainers must be laser-focused on performance and have the ability to trace all classroom activity back to the organization's goals—not in a formulaic way using MBA buzzwords, but by being ready to answer "Why are we learning this?" and explaining it in relation to the business.

I have to confess that it's easier said than done. Notwithstanding the distractions at the office such as workplace politics or cumbersome policies and processes that hang over our heads, the answer to "Why are we learning this?" can also expose uncomfortable imbalances in the tensions we explored earlier, such as whether we're more trainer-centric or more learner-centric. Or if our passion for a topic ends up influencing a pedagogical decision more than the need to meet a specific business need. Or demonstrating to the client the link between learning and business performance—that tension between being a trainer and a salesperson.

I'm not much of a numbers person. I failed math in high school, and so I get insecure when folks, such as that accountant I talked about earlier, wave a spreadsheet at me. (OK, I don't know if he was waving the spreadsheet at me—we were on the phone. But it sure felt like he was.) But accountants can offer a critical pulse check in terms of costs and benefits. While the accountant calling me about creating an elastic workforce rubbed me the wrong way, he was right in challenging me to think about the value my team brought to the organization. Organizations don't spend money on training departments for fun. They spend to be better at what they do. It's easy to forget this, especially when we find ourselves immersed in the nervous planning before a training event.

A Trainer Retools a Virtual Class on the Fly

Cindy Huggett

I FACILITATE A LOT OF VIRTUAL CLASSES and pride myself in advance preparation. I prepare my workspace, my content, and my technology, making sure I have backup plans for everything. I also prepare my participants by sending them information in advance and asking them to complete a set of preparation tasks.

Several years ago, I scheduled a virtual class with a new client. I went through my standard preparation routine, including my pre-class communication message to participants. I specifically reminded them of the virtual class parameters and the importance of not sharing computers—just one person per keyboard, please.

The day came, and it was finally time to start the virtual class. Even though I thought I was fully prepared, I soon realized things were not to go as planned.

When the virtual class began, I discovered that most participants were on their own computers as requested, but they were all sitting in the same conference room! They had gotten the message of "one person, one keyboard," except they missed the mark by not staying at their own desk, which would have ensured a truly "virtual" environment. While this situation might have been fine if I planned for it, now I was scrambling to manage the one thing I didn't plan for—a virtual class that wasn't really a virtual because all the participants were in the same room.

The situation caused immediate problems: There was a terrible sounding echo that affected our audio, and several participants had connection challenges because the site's Internet bandwidth wasn't strong enough to support them all in the room. But most importantly in my mind—the program design was going to need to change, and fast!

I needed to quickly adapt the program design. The first planned activity was to put participants into breakout groups for an icebreaker, but now the breakouts wouldn't make sense with everyone in the same physical location. Not to mention an upcoming whiteboard brainstorming activity, which works well with remote audiences but also doesn't have the same intent with everyone together.

Drawing upon my past experiences, I had to think fast and create a plan that would allow participants to still learn the content despite the unexpected circumstances. I took a deep breath and addressed the technical problems by assigning primary computers for class use and asking everyone else to disconnect. I then got everyone involved in a modified version of the icebreaker activity. As they worked together on this opening exercise, I thought through the rest of our activities to determine what needed to be adapted for the situation.

By the end, it wasn't my best class, but we made it through, and the participants learned the content. Learning a powerful lesson myself, I have since modified my pre-class communication messages. Despite the hiccups, I had a chance to flex my skills of adaptability and thinking on my feet—the key skills needed by any facilitator or trainer!

Cindy Huggett, CPLP, is author of several books on virtual training and a thought leader in our profession.

5

PLANNING ISN'T WHAT IT'S CRACKED UP TO BE

Jazz is about being in the moment.
—Herbie Hancock

IF TWO ROLES in the training world have some friction, it's trainers and instructional designers. I've heard raised voices behind closed doors and comments muttered under someone's breath as they leave a meeting. I've been copied on heated emails that would make your mother blush. And I've had to mediate a disagreement or four. While trainers in smaller organizations generally both design and facilitate learning, instructional design in larger organizations is often a separate function from facilitation. Often, the designers will sit in a different office from the facilitators. And while the tension between these two functions doesn't always bubble into the open, you'll often hear about tense meetings, such as the one I heard between Rob and Annette.

Just shy of 38 years old, Rob had clocked 15 years as a trainer, the first eight as a road warrior, delivering programs for a high-volume seminar company. Everything was tightly scripted, and he was required to deliver the same content, verbatim, every time. It was grueling work; in just one week, he might deliver full-day programs in Dallas, Houston, and Atlanta. On top of that, he was under pressure to promote the company's back-of-room sales.

So he transitioned to a corporate gig. He wanted smaller classes and the flexibility to offer more personalized workshops. He was now the senior trainer in a midsized bank that had 10 trainers and three instructional designers. But one Friday afternoon, he found himself in a conference room with Annette, the instructional designer who had just audited his session.

"Robert," she started. "You only spent 29 minutes on that conflict role-play exercise. We had allowed 35." Annette was a thorough person, and he'd noticed her following the session plan carefully, while he worked to draw the best out of the participants. "The participants knew that content," Rob said. "Remember when we did the Q&A at the start? As you saw, they nailed the 'I statements.'"

Annette had designed the program following the ADDIE model. She'd done a thorough analysis with subject matter experts across the bank and had carefully mapped out exercises she thought would most likely support each topic. She'd even done two test runs with folks from the fourth floor. How could Rob dispute that? But the real insult for Annette was that Rob hadn't set up three activities following the script she had laid out in the facilitator's guide. She'd road tested it four times with her colleagues in the ISD department, and in her mind, it was bulletproof. However, ignoring the script and using a different set of words was a conscious choice for Rob. He thought the monologue was too wordy and stilted for this group. He was trying to create an informal, conversational environment. The participants in this group were also more advanced than usual, so he worried that all the extra detail could come across as condescending.

Theirs is not the first story like this I have heard, and it shouldn't surprise us because the roles of designer and trainer are very different. If you're in a smaller organization where you do both, switching between roles is like switching between using a PC and Mac. When you look at training in larger organizations, I often find that people with certain personalities are attracted to design, while others are attracted to facilitation.

While I know we're not supposed to generalize or stereotype people, we trainers do it constantly. How often have you heard a colleague say something like, "Oh, she's an ESTJ, but super strong on the J" or "His style is dominance." We stereotype all the time, except we get fancy and use technical terms from DISC or Myers Briggs. So, acknowledging the dangers of overgeneralizing, I'm going to take a stab at stereotyping designers and trainers. The majority of instructional designers I have worked with tend to be quiet, orderly, and well planned. Many have a technical-writing background. And most trainers I have worked with are outgoing, spontaneous, and comfortable with improvisation. Yes, there are exceptions. But conduct a police lineup of trainers and designers, and I bet you can spot who the designers are, and who are trainers.

GETTING THE RELATIONSHIP RIGHT

Not all organizations manage to find the right balance between the instructional design and learning delivery teams. One organization that has is Ellie Mae, a mortgage software company located just outside San Francisco. Marc Wilner, the manager of enterprise education, says a number of things make for a successful ISD–trainer relationship.

"At a manager level, we work hard to ensure we have the same philosophy," he said. "Our trainers are steeped in an active learning approach that is less reliant on PowerPoint. We've worked hard to ensure our design team understands our preferences."

He said that trainers need to be involved with designers all through the design process. "I've worked in companies where designers don't talk to trainers unless they're the subject matter expert. They then dump the participant guide and slide deck on them and effectively wipe their hands.

"We like designers to sit in on the classes as we trial them so they can experience what we're doing and see how it works. Their feedback is valuable, as are the insights we share that they would not be exposed to at their desks; they discover stuff they'd only learn in the classroom."

I like how Marc talks about "trialing" the programs. A lot of people talk about dress rehearsals, which is more performance language from the theater. But then Marc is switched on about learning.

"[Designers] like us to sit with them when planning activities and other learning strategies," he said. "They like to hear our insights into what works and doesn't in the nitty gritty of the classroom. And they challenge our ideas, too, which strengthens our practice.

"We are also very committed to the ideas that learning doesn't happen on slides. And through the relationship we have built, we're able to share our preference for active learning, which allows for trainers to make tailored modifications as they teach to further drive the learning home."

Marc said that the best way to ensure an effective relationship between trainers and designers is communication. "It has to happen before, during, and after the development of a course," he explained. "Both roles bring important perspectives to helping learners learn skills."

I think Marc and the crew at Ellie Mae have nailed this. Because where I've seen the tension most is when designers expect trainers to stick rigidly to their script or to never deviate from their slide deck. And delivering content, which we know will mostly be forgotten, becomes more important than stepping out of the way of the learners to help them build learning.

The Challenges of Instructional Design

The challenge with getting instructional design right is that it makes assumptions about learners and the classroom that are hard to predict. It doesn't matter how good your lesson plan or script is; stuff goes wrong. And despite the nifty lists in industry magazines of what to do before you start training, your preparation will very often fail to prepare you and you'll have to improvise. Trainers of all experience levels have war stories where the air conditioner failed, they had to teach a class on Internet skills but the Internet didn't work, or the participant guides were sent to the wrong building.

As we discussed in chapter 2, each learner in a class will process new information by drawing on personal memories that can be very different from those of the trainer and others in the group. From these memories, people form mental models and develop mindsets to understand the world and process learning. So it makes sense that with a little research, we can find out their background and structure the experience using the appropriate language for learners and develop activities, analogies, and other strategies that will resonate with them.

However, we don't always know who will be in a class. Late registrations, poor administration, or simply lack of time to contact participants beforehand means that we frequently don't find out people's backgrounds until they walk through the door. But their background, such as their role or training, can have a huge impact on how they approach learning. For example, lawyers see things very differently from marketers and will solve a problem using very different approaches. I don't want to oversimplify, but lawyers are generally conditioned to look for risk because their job is protecting clients, whereas marketers look for opportunities because they're trained to look for more revenue. If you're running a class on emotional intelligence, which is relevant to many professionals, and you know most of the participants will be either lawyers or marketers, should you structure the learning to play to the lawyer's mindset, or the marketer's? Do you create reflection exercises that draw on the risk or opportunity approach? And which profession do you draw analogies or metaphors from? In most situations, the dynamics will be subtler, but I think it's unreasonable to expect the instructional designer to really know who is going to walk in that door.

Another unpredictability is that pesky little issue of disruptive participants. It only takes one person who talks too long, tells an inappropriate joke, or has a problem with technology to burn an hour of time that was allocated for something specific. The trainer must then rework the plan and skip some exercises or condense them on the run. I'm familiar with workshops that have been closed a day early due to issues with one participant, which led facilitators to be concerned for the safety of other participants. I often ask in my train-the-trainer workshops for examples of disruptions. One disruption that I have often heard and hope never to experience personally is someone vomiting in class, sometimes on another participant. I'm not kidding. I can almost hear you exclaim "Eeeewwww." But hey, it happens. And you can never predict when.

If it's not unpredictable people, it's an unpredictable venue. I was hired to work with military trainers a few years ago at a location that doesn't appear on the map. To get to the training venue, I had to drive down a dirt ride with signs that said, "Beware, unexploded ordinances." (That's one way to raise your cortisol levels.) I had asked that the room be set up in rounds to promote collaborative learning. But the people who managed the building changed my room at the last minute, so I walked into a room where desks were arranged theater style. Trainers are encouraged to move desks around to create the right atmosphere, except when I went to shift the first table, it wouldn't budge and I almost broke my back. The desks were bolted to the floor.

Taking this a step further, I had a fire alarm go off when facilitating ATD's Master Trainer Program in Washington, D.C. Sixty people were enrolled, and I was one of four trainers, so we each took a group of 15. The program was scheduled at a brand-new hotel, but the hotel wasn't open because its opening had been delayed. Hotel management promised the meeting rooms would be ready, because the rooms had been booked a year in advance and we were relying on them. What the hotel didn't tell us—or perhaps they didn't know—was that fire marshals were testing the fire alarms on the first day. Every 10 minutes, for a whole day, the sirens would wail. There is no way you can follow the lesson plan in those circumstances. None. So I dropped the script. And I dropped the PowerPoints. I looked at the learning objectives and figured out a way to cover them with what I had.

Because of all this, we were moved across the street to the Walter E. Washington Convention Center the next day. Only the city decided to dig up the sewers that day, and all we heard that morning was the noise of jackhammers. You can't make this stuff up. Participants could hardly hear me and to be honest, I couldn't hear myself think!

Sometimes things go as planned, but very often they don't. I don't know how Annette would have felt if it was her program I dumped because of the jackhammer. But a trainer's job is to respond in the moment and help create an environment where learners can be comfortable, safe, and focused on the learning objectives. Managers who send their staff to our programs don't do so because they want to hear us read from a script and stick with it no matter what's going on in the environment. They want their people to leave with real skills.

Anyway, despite these challenges, the ATD Education folks pulled off a few miracles and it all ended well. But I discovered something really interesting. The class got some of the best feedback I can remember. One of the participants was a senior trainer at major restaurant chain with 20 years' experience. He signed up for the program to freshen his skills, and, like many folks who attend my programs, could himself teach me a lot about training. He said when I left "the script" and allowed the group and circumstances to influence the training, the experience was inspiring. Instead of trusting my script, I trusted the learners. They had the resources to build their learning whether or not I followed the script. It reminded me of the software training in Lincoln, Nebraska. When I stopped trying so hard to follow my plan for teaching the video editing program and trusted the learners to draw on their own resources to play and tinker with the content, the learning was deeper.

The Shortcomings of No Instructional Design

Do you think I'm weaving a masterful argument to say we should ditch instructional design? Not at all. Implementing a rigorous ISD process was one of my priorities when the BBC first hired me to manage its New Media Training Unit. It's just that having worked as both a designer and trainer, I think we need to find the right balance. Annette's work in preparing the class beats anything a trainer might do on the spot. But the instant it becomes an exercise of reciting a script, like an actor performs a play, it's no longer about the learner—it's about the show. However, avoiding this rigidity and opting for an approach where there is no planning and it's all situational is no good either. Preparation is what gives a trainer the edge to be agile.

There are a few circumstances in which I think trainers should closely follow a script. One is when you're teaching compliance topics or legal matters because there are legal responsibilities to deliver certain messages. Another is when the trainer is a rookie. It's a seductive idea to think that anyone with the ability to speak and be confident in front of a group of people will make a good trainer. But like with every job, it takes years and thousands of hours of practice to truly develop skills to be fully competent. Trainers need the freedom to adjust content and activities to better suit the unique needs of people in the group. They have the experience, skills, and confidence to make activities and discussions more relevant based on what they see in classroom interactions to better align the many unpredictable variables with the goal of helping people learn new skills. However, when the trainer does not have these skills, and this is most often in the first few years of their training career, I think it's unreasonable to put the pressure on them to make these adjustments when they already have enough other things to worry about. I think seminar companies understand this when they hire new trainers, because many demand that they strictly follow the session plans without allowing a minute more or less for activities or predetermined discussions. One training company writes all its session plans so "any idiot can teach them." I won't tell you the company because it is too well known. The problem is that I know this company also hires many seasoned, top-notch trainers who would deliver unbeatable learning experiences if they were allowed.

So, going back to Rob and Annette, who is right and who is wrong? Or is that the wrong question?

The Designer and the Trainer Can Be Friends

What does it mean to have an effective relationship between trainers and designers? Perhaps the first step is developing a consensus around the purpose of the program as expressed through learning objectives. The objectives should be the core contract with the learner. Understanding that objectives are what the designer is designing for and the trainer is facilitating for allows each the freedom to be good at their respective roles.

Instructional designers are focused on preparing the best materials to support the learning. But it's an entirely unreasonable expectation that they can predict every classroom experience. Who could predict turning up to a Russian workshop and being told you are now teaching revenue flows rather than storytelling? How can an instructional designer plan for a disruptive participant who sucks the oxygen out of a classroom? Or know the experience level and memories a learner will pull on to make sense of the content? Sure, many of these things can be surveyed, but many participants have an overinflated or underinflated sense of their skill level. It's unreasonable for us to expect that instructional designers can predict which curveballs might be thrown to the trainer in the classroom.

Rigid lesson plans or scripts may hinder rather than help learning. Trainers need some flexibility. But how much flex is too much? Winging it is certainly not acceptable. One of the professors in my undergraduate studies defined pedagogy as the "art and science of teaching." The answer to this may fall more in the art of facilitation than the science.

As an art form, jazz offers a model we might consider for training. It's different from classical music because it relies on improvisation, whereas classical music has every note written down. Both forms of music have plenty of room for creativity and self-expression. But jazz achieves it by allowing the artist to improvise around a melody and chord progression. Every performance is unique and personal, while still being true to the original intent. So if Duke Ellington plays the old jazz standard "Satin Doll," it will certainly sound similar to when Bill Evans plays it. But it will be different and uniquely reflect his feelings and the feelings of his audience and venue.

Learning objectives are like the chord progression and melody. In my mind the objectives are non-negotiable, representing the intention of the learning and making the desired results very clear. The melody, meanwhile, represents how the learning is achieved. And just as a jazz composer plans the melody, the performer is free to improvise around the melody by adding tone and spontaneity in response to who's in the room and other circumstances that are impossible to predict.

I must confess. I don't much like following session plans word for word and sticking to rigid timing when they were designed by someone at a desk in a building far away from the classroom and all the unpredictable variables it brings, even if that person was me. And I don't like walking into a classroom without a plan and clear set of objectives. My commitment is to help learners perform the objectives when they leave the class, not sit and watch me perform a script. But without an outline based on the well-written objectives—a chord progression—it is very tough to help learners achieve their goals.

I love committing to the learning objective and using the activities with the freedom to adapt to the needs of the learner. When I set up the instructional design process for the BBC's New Media Training Unit almost 20 years ago, my team created what we called a "curriculum pack" for every single course. In it, we listed the learning objective. Then for each objective, we suggested activities that we had found were helpful to teaching that objective. But we said to the trainer that they had to help participants achieve the objective, not do the activity. If they found another activity that better played to participants in the room, we'd trust their professionalism to make that decision. We also provided further resources and lists of best practice. But inherent in the planning we did was that we trusted the trainer to be agile and change things based on what happened in the classroom.

I suppose when I say that planning isn't what it's cracked up to be, I really mean that *rigid* planning isn't. But when planning allows for flexibility, the partnership between instructional designers and trainers can be incredibly rewarding.

6

PLAN TO DUMP YOUR PLAN, BUT NEVER LEAVE HOME WITHOUT IT

If you fail to plan, you are planning to fail.
—Benjamin Franklin

I WAS 4,506 MILES FROM HOME. Fifteen managers sat in front of me, at narrow, slightly yellow desks covered in Formica. Like many European buildings built in the last 40 years, this one had lovely big windows. And the training room was bathed in a golden light, which warmed the space. Although the atmosphere was decidedly chilly.

We were 90 minutes into a workshop on how to lead change, and they had not laughed at one of my jokes. Not that I'm necessarily funny, but I usually get a giggle or two, even if just out of sympathy. And except for the first 15 minutes, when things seemed to be comfortable, they had effectively gone mute. Participants weren't answering questions. They didn't give me eye contact, nor to each other. They were all fluent in English—I'd chatted comfortably with most of them before the class started—so it wasn't that either.

I had been cautious about agreeing to do this. To fly from Washington, D.C., to Zagreb, in Croatia, for a one-day workshop was a big undertaking. Before I work on change programs for private clients, I like to learn about the company's culture and their change plans. The kind of things I'm talking about are beyond what you'll read in their annual report and more like what you'll hear whispered around the watercooler. I like to know if the reorganization has been announced to the staff, how the workforce has reacted to the proposed changes, where the leaders in my workshop stand on their role, and what sorts of obstacles they foresee. I also expect participants to have read and digested the change plan, even if only an executive summary. So, I quizzed the HR director over Skype and included in my agreement that all participants would have been given the change plan to read before the workshop. With all that settled, I planned the one-day workshop roughly following the ADDIE model, tailoring it to what I knew about their corporate culture.

On the morning of training, I met with the managing director an hour and a half ahead of the 9:30 session. He was a nice chap and was glad I'd flown over from Washington. I asked him about the workplace culture, if the participants had been briefed, and what their reactions were. All standard stuff, really. He said he wasn't sure what their reactions were, but they had all been briefed.

Now I stood in front of a bunch of managers who were totally disengaged. It was getting close to the break time, so I suggested that we have coffee with the hopes that it would at least increase their energy levels. Most sprung up, grabbed coffees, and headed outside to drink their beverage and smoke cigarettes. The company had allocated Antun, a manager, to accompany me during my time there. Rather than grab the coffee in the classroom where they'd placed an urn and some cookies, we headed for the company's cafeteria.

"Antun," I asked. "These folks seem really quiet—is that normal?" I'd previously done work for two media companies in Croatia, and the participants had been very engaging, so I was sure it wasn't a cultural thing. "No," he said. "Usually these folks are quite animated. I think they were shell-shocked by your opening comments."

Who's in Control?

A lot of trainers blame themselves when a group lacks energy or folks hold back from engaging in exercises or discussions. They think they gave the instructions incorrectly or asked poorly phrased questions. Trainers tell me all the time that they feel this pressure and if I'm honest, I still feel that way sometimes. When this happens, they respond by becoming more animated, speaking louder, walking around the room, and using exaggerated gestures. Kind of like mashing the keys on your keyboard to revive your frozen computer—they're searching for the right button, any button, to press to bring the class back to life. It's all based on the assumption that trainers should have control, and in fact can.

However, we have much less control than we think. Throwing our hands around and becoming more animated usually makes only us feel better. In the classroom, we cannot completely control our participants' motivation, thoughts, actions, interactions. Old school trainers don't always agree with me on this. But think about it from a situation outside the classroom. It was on the tarmac, leaving Washington, D.C., for Zagreb. I was in an aisle seat on the red eye to Frankfurt, my first stop, on a United Boeing 777. The captain turned on the PA and got ready to tell us about the flight. Keep your seat belt on, use the restrooms in your ticketed cabin, and all that stuff. Bear in mind that this was about eight years ago, because he also said, "And we've closed the plane's door; please turn off all cell phones." The captain is in charge of the flight, passenger safety, and responding to problems. I looked across the aisle to a gentleman in his mid-40s, and he was busily searching the Internet on his phone. I have lost count of how many times I saw this during that year. (Errr, or how many times I did it myself.) The captain of an aircraft can't even control what his passengers do when the instruction is ostensibly tied to safety. What makes trainers think they have that sort of control in the classroom?

In that Zagreb classroom, I had no control over whether the participants would engage in group discussion.

When I was planning this book, I sat in a café and jotted down who controls different things in the classroom. The trainer controls what time she turns up, what she says, what slides she presents, and the activities or discussions she asks people to take part in. Sometimes she controls the content (although often it's controlled by the instructional designer.) But she doesn't control whether someone checks their Twitter feed or email during a class, or what memories participants draw on to make sense of what you say. Or their emotions: Are participants excited or bored by the class? The trainer can't control whether participants had enough sleep the night before, or if they had a row with their spouse that overshadows anything you're teaching. There is more that we can't control than we can.

When the Proverbial Hits the Fan

What trainers do have, though, is influence. Unfortunately influence doesn't always help. How could my influence persuade these learners in Zagreb to take part in the discussion? Was there a magic button? The issues of control and predictability are worth considering when it comes to planning. Ben Franklin says we're planning to fail when we don't plan, but much of what we plan in today's world is based on industrial notions of predictability and command and control hierarchal structures. How can we plan for every dynamic? Every person in the class brings different experiences to draw on when they build their learning off what you say and the discussions and exercises they participate in. Every group is different. Some are loud, others are quiet; some have disruptive folks, others are made up of people who are distracted. The politics vary from person to person, from group to group. What agendas do individuals bring to training? The location where training is conducted can have a huge impact: Are there windows? Is the room too crowded? Is there enough light? Does the air conditioning work in the afternoon, as the sun beams into the room? Organizational culture affects learning, too—and not just between different companies, but within them. A class with salespeople will be different from a class of accountants. It's just not effective to deliver the exact same program in the same way to different groups of people. To the new trainer, these variables can seem worrying. But to me, they make our work interesting and exciting because you can never predict them. No matter how much data you gather from conversations or pre-class questionnaires to build a general picture, you can never fully know until you're in the room learning about the learners. No matter what people tell you.

And this is where I was in Zagreb. I couldn't force the participants to be animated or take part in discussions. I could jump around the room, become more animated, talk louder, and hope that they'd be interested. But they had the control over their participation, not me. I asked Antun what he meant by shell-shocked, because I didn't recall saying anything out of order. "I guess, Jonathan," he said, "that no one has told them about the reorganization."

Shut the front door. A key part of my agreement was that each person would be given the change plan to read and be able to ask questions, if necessary. And the managing director had told me to my face at 8 that morning that each participant knew about it. Was he mistaken? Had he lied to me? Unfortunately, I couldn't be distracted by that question right now, because I needed to figure out what to do. These folks had found out from the guy in a suit from Washington that a reorganization was happening. They had no idea about their future, because no one had briefed them on the change and how it would affect them and their teams. And being Friday, they'd go home to their families thinking that their jobs were on the line. I felt horrible for them.

These sorts of things can happen often. In another gig, I was asked to facilitate a weeklong strategy session for a global publishing company developing a talent strategy. Working with another consultant, we met with the CEO, and over six weeks we fine-tuned the scope and outcomes. The company signed off, and we agreed to conduct the session in the Middle East. When we arrived in their boardroom on Sunday morning, which is the first day of the week there, the executives proceeded to present their talent strategy. They had completed everything we had been hired to help them with. I looked at my plan for the next four days, considered that I had spent two days and half of my plane trip preparing, and quietly packed it back in my briefcase. "So, how will we spend this week, Mr. Jonathan?" the executives asked. Didn't Franklin say that if I fail to plan, I plan to fail? Well, I had planned everything following standard practice in our profession and still thought that I was about to fail. Why did they sign off on work for us to do when they'd already done it? I just didn't get it.

Cut Yourself Some Slack

If there's anything I've learned over the years, it's that more often than not, the sessions I plan turn out differently because I simply can't predict all these variables. At first, I used to think that I was failing in my pre-analysis. But experience showed me that the more wedded I was to my plan—the one I designed at my desk in my Washington office, based on surveys and phone and email interviews, where I couldn't meet the participants and see which were introverts or extroverts, which would want more breaks, or whether the room had sun shining in after lunch that puts people to sleep—the more difficult it was for me to create an experience that helps learners build their learning. As such, I've come to never expect my planning to turn out. I might plan a series of exercises, but there's a fire alarm and I lose two hours. I once ran a video workshop in Boston, and the UPS guy couldn't find someone at the venue the day before to sign the receipt slip when delivering the video cameras. So the cameras were sent back to Washington, and I had to redesign the class without cameras on day 1. One corporate client had me change rooms three times in two days because the chief operating officer decided to commandeer the training room for executive meetings.

If we can't predict these things, should we just spend our prep time doing something else and plan to wing it when we get on-site? Only if you have to step in at the last minute or the client imposes a new agenda on you as you walk in the room do you have the excuse to wing it. Failing to plan in any other situation amounts to professional malpractice. So how do we prepare if we don't know what to expect?

I think it's about focusing on the right things in planning and creating space to change what you're doing. To deliver transformative learning that has real impact, trainers need to be agile. And they need to plan their session with the room to respond to learners needs—needs that are not always easy to predict until you meet in person. What does this all mean in the classroom? And how did I pull off the Friday training session in Zagreb? *Did* I pull it off? Let's first look at developing agility, and then discuss some practical thoughts about preparation.

Agility Is What Separates Novices From Master Trainers

I've been facilitating ATD's Master Trainer Program almost since it was launched, and I often find folks asking about the difference between a novice and master trainer. My thought is that the master trainer has agility. In pragmatic terms, the novice trainer presents content, following a session plan. Every decision he makes as he teaches is about presenting the content along the lines of the session plan. Sometimes he'll be focused on reciting the exact same stories in the exact same way every time. His session plan—or more aptly, his script—is his crutch. If something goes wrong—maybe a participant disrupts the class, or some folks have difficulty grasping a complex issue—he will try and coerce the group back to the slides or participant guide. The content and session plan are what determines whether the training is successful. However, a master trainer is focused on the business needs and learning objectives. She worries whether the participants will be able to perform the task they came to learn, not whether she followed the script correctly. She'll change the stories to make them more relevant or slow the pace, so it's easier to practice. And she'll have the confidence to do it.

What does this look like in slightly more philosophical terms? In 2017, *Inc.* magazine described what it considers to be the top three traits of agile leaders (Pruitt 2017). That article really stuck out to me, and I've been thinking about how it can be instructive to adapt them for the trainer. To that end, an agile trainer needs to have clarity, connection, and confidence.

Clarity

Leaders, *Inc.* says, have clarity in the face of complex change. For trainers, this clarity comes from knowing the business need the session has been planned to address. This is usually expressed by the specific learning objectives. When something changes—a participant hijacks a class, or folks turn up without having completed the pre-work—the agile trainer will change what was planned to support the learners and where they're at. But they don't just change on a whim. They use the learning objective as a yardstick to determine how and what to change and keep things on track.

Agile trainers talk differently from novice trainers. Novices will say that they can cover material, like a colleague of mine in Paris who told a client, "I have a slide deck that can cover that topic for you." In contrast, agile trainers will talk about the tasks that learners can perform after a workshop. That's their focus. And as novice trainers will try and fit the class to the presentation, agile trainers will change whatever they need to help the learner perform the learning objective.

Connection

The article says that the connection trait is about heart and emotional intelligence. It is equally critical for the agile trainer. Agile trainers understand people. They know how to read folks, listen to them, respond to them, and influence them. For example, a novice trainer will give a presentation at 3 p.m. even if participants look dog-tired, because his goal is to deliver the content. An agile trainer will know that just presenting content does not lead to learning, and that when participants are tired, their memory consolidation and reaction times drop. She will see people's energy levels lagging. She's not worried about whether the content was delivered—she's worried that the participants will learn. And rather than waste their time with content they'll quickly forget, she suggests they adjourn for the day and come back fresher the next day.

Confidence

Leaders need to lead through uncertainty in today's post-industrial workplace and must often do so without the information and data they need to make important decisions. *Inc.* magazine says that this requires guts. For trainers, it's the guts to change something you're doing in class that was not planned, often when you're not 100 percent sure it's the best way to help learners hit their learning objective. This confidence is made easier when you have total clarity of the learning objective, and the emotional stamina to support and respond to learners as they work through a change or uncertain experiences. For example, you come across a roadblock in class: Perhaps there's a hidden agenda among some participants or a misunderstanding about the purpose of the class. The master trainer will stop and process it, much like author Elaine Biech does in her spotlight on page 85, when she turned a leadership workshop into a career development day to better prepare the participants for major change.

An Agile Trainer Still Needs to Come Prepared

There's a subtle difference between how a novice and agile trainer prepares for a workshop. The novice trainer spends the bulk of his time on what he does and how he presents, like agonizing over crafting the most delightful-looking PowerPoint slides, or practicing how he delivers certain stories. He'll make sure his props and training aids are packed in the order he follows on his session plan. As a result, it will most likely be a great presentation, although participants may forget most of it. The agile trainer, however, will be more focused on what she's going to get the learners to do. She'll be more concerned about how she gets the learners talking, rather than how well she transitions between slides. She'll be more concerned about ensuring that the props are in place that learners can use to experiment or practice the tasks they're learning. Her focus is on getting the participants to do the work of learning—deliberate practice. That's what leads to retention. She'll spend more time researching the folks who are coming to class and devote considerable cognitive effort in the first couple of hours to listening to participants and learning their needs.

So, what does this look like? Rather than do this from an instructional design perspective, let's consider some of the general concepts, based on our need to be learner-centered. There are plenty of great books on ISD with even more extensive lists, so I'm going to focus on the things I think are important.

What to Prepare

Here's what you should always prepare beforehand:

- **Learn the tasks you're going to help people learn.** This means being clear about what people need to know and do to perform them successfully. Practice the tasks you'll be teaching so you can be confident sharing them, understand where some folks might struggle, and have remedies ready. Knowing the tasks well is a great way to reduce nerves in the classroom.

- **Find out who will be in the class and why they are there.** What business need is the class going to solve? If you're a contractor and doing an on-site session for a corporate client, find out their organizational culture. Is there a common time they take lunch? Will they eat at the cafeteria? Do they like to start early?

- **Check in to be sure that participants are clear about any pre-work they need to complete.** Make sure that they understand your expectations. If you're an internal trainer and have easy access to their manager, send them an email to give them a heads-up of what's expected. Ask the manager to discuss how participants will put the training into action when they return to the job.

- **Brainstorm learning methods that will most effectively help learners understand and remember the tasks.** Think through their sequence and how to set them up so that learners can follow easily.
- **Create a rough outline for your workshop.** Everyone has a preference for what this looks like. Some people do a running list, others a clock. I draw a mind map of how I think the class will go. Visual outlines make it easier for me to jump around and respond to learner needs.
- **Plan learning aids.** Produce or gather videos, slides, music, and other content and load it on your laptop. Label files clearly so you don't get lost when trying to find them. I tend to make a desktop shortcut to the folder with digital content.
- **Pack your gear.** That includes your laptop; a portable speaker if you use videos and music, just in case there isn't one at the venue; and all the accessories, like power cables. Make sure you have a copy of your session outline, a facilitator guide if you have one, and the participant guide.

When to Prepare

I don't think there's any hard and fast rule about when to prepare other than do it as soon as you have what you need. Some trainers will demand six weeks' notice before they facilitate a program, whereas others will walk into a virtual or physical classroom at the drop of a hat. It doesn't seem to make much difference whether they're internal or external trainers. One of the things I have found helpful is to have a checklist of what needs to be done and when, so that prep follows a workflow. It will look different for each person. The following are a few quick things I've learned through experience.

Book your travel as soon as you can, especially if it's international. The more time you have, the more options you have to chart the most direct route. In chapter 10, we talk about choosing flights and booking hotels. If your boss is sending you to another country, you may need time to get visas and vaccinations. Visas to some countries can take you a whole day, requiring you to line up at the consulate. Sometimes you can use visa companies to get things done quickly for you, but if your company won't pay for that, put a day aside to line up at the consulate and find a good book to read. There may be protocols you need to follow as well, such as contacting certain people in the host country.

You'll need to be sure that workbooks and job aids are ready for distribution. If you're training at a location away from your office, companies such as Mimeo have made life much easier because you can order workbooks the day before and they'll arrive on-site by 8 a.m. the following day. But order them several weeks before, and you'll save money. It's important to check with your client or the coordinator at the location where you'll train about where to get the books and when. Their office may not be at the training center, and even if books arrive the day before, they may not have planned to stop by their office. Alternatively, they may be coordinating a lot of training and ask you not to send the workbooks too far in advance simply because they only have so much desk space. I've delivered programs in large warehouses where workbooks and learning materials turn up a couple of days early but somehow at the wrong door, and it takes forever to track them down. Check these things with whoever is coordinating the training on-site. If you're delivering a workshop in the building where your desk is, still take care of all these things early—you don't want to be running around on the morning of a workshop doing last-minute photocopying. And if you're working from home base, you can set the room up the day before.

Sometimes you'll be delivering a workshop for a whole team. Talk with their manager early about what you expect from them in terms of pre-work, and what they can expect from you. Discuss some of the logistics we've already talked about. What time can you get into the room? How would you like it set up? When do they want breaks? Set a timeline for when you need answers to these questions and actions to be completed. For example, if they're booking your travel, tell them when you need it. If they're handling registrations, tell them when you need the list of participants. If participants need to complete a questionnaire or pre-work, discuss when you need this done.

The logistics are the most important thing to focus on in preparation. You want to be sure you'll turn up on time, the workbooks and other learning materials are there, and participants are there. Start doing logistics as soon as you can, namely when training is confirmed. Agility in the classroom becomes difficult when logistics aren't properly prepared because they distract you from responding to learners and their needs, which very often you won't learn about until they walk in the door.

IT'S LIKE A PREZI

One of the recent presentation applications that's growing in popularity is the Prezi app. Rather than present information in a linear fashion, such as with PowerPoint or Keynote, it offers you a way to dip in and out of the presentation in any order that you like. It might be the order you like at the time, or in a learning environment, the order that best fits a class conversation or discussion. Prezi, or similar flexible presentation software, can be an agile trainer's lifeline. I see Prezi as an ideal metaphor for flexible session plans. As trainers, we can adapt to what participants need to learn in a way that best suits the group, the location, and the business need.

Adapting on the Fly in Zagreb

Planning is critical. But it's how we plan that's important. We need to plan in a way that gives us the ultimate flexibility to help learners learn the tasks, generally expressed as learning objectives. The reason we need this flexibility is that we can never be sure what will present itself when you arrive in the classroom. Like me in Zagreb.

I'd taken on the gig, as a training consultant, on the condition that I not be the one who tells them about the change. Philosophically, that's not a conversation I believe should be left to an external consultant. The leadership needed to do that, even if the consultant guided how they would do it. They had not done what we agreed, and quite possibly the managing director had lied to me during my 8 a.m. meeting. I was in an uncomfortable position.

In addition, it was a Friday, and folks were going home to a weekend of uncertainty. It was easy for me—I was flying back to Washington that night. How could I salvage this? I thought the fact they had not informed their managers about the change was a breach of our contract, so I stopped the class. And I asked them to tell me the biggest challenge they faced in their roles. They talked about nurturing innovation in their teams. So, I redesigned the workshop and taught them an innovation formula I had developed for another workshop. Participants had little appetite to learn about the grief cycle or Kotter's 8-Step Change Model, but were clearly motivated about spurring on the creative spirit in their teams. So, 4,506 miles from home, we made the class about what would help them.

A Trainer Responds to a Communication Curveball

Elaine Biech

IT WAS EARLY IN MY CAREER as a training consultant, and my largest and most prominent global client was bringing me in on a regular basis to teach "communication skills"—you know—listen to understand, communicate with diplomacy, influence others, and manage conflict. On this particular cloudy day in October, I was scheduled to work with a group of 18 guys from the factory and came prepared for their good-natured humor and semi-inappropriate jokes.

We started on time, even though several of the men showed up uncharacteristically late. I tossed out my best one-liners and received no reaction. They moved into the small groups and completed the tasks, but they seemed to be in an unusually subdued mood. When seated in the U-shape, normally best for creating informal discussion, the participants gazed at the table.

Due to a lack of participation, we reached the break much earlier than the scheduled time. Instead of pushing forward I decided these guys needed some coffee and sugar, so we paused for the break. But even the break seemed abnormal: no jokes about my height, no loud stories about their weekend activities, and no questions about whether we would end early. Strange. I decided something unusual had happened.

Once the donuts were all scarfed up and everyone had returned to the room, I pulled a chair into the center of the group and sat down—something I never do when facilitating a group. I noticed some uncomfortable shuffling and all eyes staring at the tables. I plunged in with, "Something is going on. I am obviously not meeting your needs and want to know what I can do to change that."

At that point, most volunteered comments, and I quickly learned that everyone in the session was about to be laid off. This workshop was management's way of supporting employees by giving them something they thought would be helpful.

What to do. I had two clients: the HR director who wrote my checks and this room full of dejected employees. Yep, I might irritate the check writer and he might never invite me back. On the other hand, I had 18 unhappy participants who were going on unemployment the following week. I considered for about 10 seconds and then opted for the only decision that was right in my mind. I gave them a quick five-minute stand-up-stretch break and reimagined an agenda that would meet their needs. Upon their return, we practiced writing resumes, role-played job interviews, brainstormed companies that might have job openings, discussed how to request references, and more.

I left the day, thinking about the lessons I learned; there were three:

- Check with your client by asking, "has anything changed since we last spoke?"
- Attend to your instincts early.
- And most important, know your clients and what they really need—no matter who is paying you.

Elaine Biech is author of Washington Post *#1 bestseller nonfiction book* The Art and Science of Training, *and more than 70 books on training.*

7

IT'S NOT JUST WHAT *YOU* DO

There is a deep interconnectedness of all life on Earth, from the tiniest
organisms to the largest ecosystems, and absolutely between each person.
—*Bryant McGill*

THE MAASAI MARA is home to one of nature's great annual events. At the beginning of the dry season, tens of thousands of wildebeest journey from the Serengeti in Tanzania, where the grass dries up, to the Maasai Mara in Kenya, where it is green and plentiful. Wildebeest are ugly animals, with heads like buffalos and hinds like horses, but they're brave because their annual pilgrimage is incredibly dangerous. To reach the fertile pastures, they must cross the crocodile-infested Mara River.

The crossing is not pretty. As the wildebeest wait to cross, the crocs wait patiently below. The wildebeest are heading to the grassy Mara for food, but many will become food for the crocodiles. This is one of the more grizzly of nature's ecological patterns, forming what scientists call an ecosystem. Not all ecosystems may seem as grizzly but up close, every part of the system lives in constant tension with other parts of the system. One thing changes, and it has a knock-on effect. That's because an ecosystem is a dynamic system of organisms that interact and create a sort of equilibrium.

Each dynamic has its own set of complexities and works together, each tiny component acting and reacting as it thirsts for equilibrium through a self-regulating and self-sustaining process. This is what happened with Ghost and Darkness, notorious African lions in the 19th century. Something changed in their ecosystem that turned them into man-eaters. This is what scared me, lying in a tent somewhere in the Maasai Mara.

The week before I'd run a leadership program with a colleague for newspaper editors in Nairobi, the capital of Kenya. Our wives had flown in from America to join us for a safari, and I was looking forward to what promised to be a life-changing experience. Instead, I was sick—out of action for four days. My illness was punctuated only by my wife returning to our tent from safari to describe the amazing ways the animals and ecological systems played with one other, and a daily visit from the local doctor to assure me I didn't have malaria. I shared with the doctor, a Kenyan man in his mid-30s, my one concern about going on safari: "I don't want to be eaten by a lion." I'd seen TV shows, you know.

"Lions don't tend to eat humans," he said. He had that reassuring doctorly manner. "They go for zebra, gazelle, and buffalo." He was right in general, because I later looked it up, being that nervous type who needs a second opinion when it comes to scary animals in countries I was a stranger to. But the good doctor didn't mention a famous exception. In 1898, British colonists were building a railway in Kenya, and two lions, Ghost and Darkness, were reported to have picked off up to 135 people. Why did these lions eat humans when they normally prefer a buffalo ribeye? Did they just change their preference, or did something happen to their DNA? Scientists say that most animals have an instinctive aversion to humans—it's a survival thing. We're an unknown quantity and as such, a threat. It would be easy to analyze the incident in isolation, a one-off occurrence not connected to anything else. But events like these happen within a bigger context, and looking for the pattern can be more instructive. There were few forensic tools in the 1800s to be totally sure why they changed menus, but a massive outbreak of rinderpest swept through the area at about the same time. Rinderpest is a nasty disease that causes fever, discharge, and dehydration, and can kill an animal in 10 to 15 days. And this outbreak decimated the population of gazelles, zebras, and buffalo—the lions' regular prey. They had to find a new food source and so, in desperation, they turned to humans. Of course, there are some added complexities involved, but suffice it to say that one change created a knock-on effect with real-world, life-threatening results.

The amazing Maasai Mara is not the only ecosystem. We live and work in one too.

The Delicate Ecosystem of Workplace Learning

Ecosystem as a term is increasingly being used as a metaphor to explain the broader context of workplace learning. It's really helpful because learning has been traditionally seen as an event in a classroom. Thus, companies and business managers analyze the success or failure of training on what happened in the classroom. Have you ever had a call from a manager who says, "I thought you taught them how to use XYZ software. They can't use it!" You're left there scratching your head, thinking, *They did pretty well in class.* While training often gets the blame, the reality is that what we do exists as part of the larger ecosystem in which workers learn, and factors outside the classroom often have a bigger impact on the success or failure of learning. And these are the factors we have little control over.

About 10 years ago, a training company I ran in London did some work for a major national newspaper. We were hired to help print journalists make video packages. We followed the ADDIE process for design and included lots of deliberate practice. At the end of three days, the newspaper reporters were producing respectable video packages. Overall, the workshops were great, and the editor in chief was impressed when he saw what they'd made during the class. But a few weeks later, he called to tell me the quality of videos on their website had not improved. Was his training spend a waste?

No one likes those phone calls. So, I asked to talk with a sample of the participants. It turned out that two crusty old news desk editors had put the screws on reporters who wanted to do video and gave them assignments that did not allow them to produce video packages. For some reason, the editors didn't like video. Maybe they were threatened by the world of the new. At any rate, it was two or three weeks before the reporters had a chance to make a video, but by then they had forgotten much of what they'd learned.

There was little performance improvement, but it had nothing to do with the class. It was influenced by something out there in the ecosystem. And news editors, or managers in other situations, are not the only forces in a system that can make a training investment a waste of time. Poor resources, no time to practice, budget decisions, work events: We could build a long list. Thinking of what we do as being one part of the ecosystem is incredibly helpful because we can see that training success is not down to us. I shudder to think, early in my career, how much stock I put into giving perfect presentations given that so little of it was remembered and thus failed to prepare learners to use their skills in the real world. The reality is that we're just a cog in the wheel. Just as one event in the wild can cause animals to change their historic eating patterns, one small change in the workplace can derail the effort you put into a perfect learning solution.

Making Sense of the Learning Ecosystem

The first writer I read who used *ecosystem* as a metaphor was David Kelly from the eLearning Guild, back in 2013. He contended that we've "torn down the walls of the classroom and realized that learning happens all the time, in just about all areas of an organization, and in formal and informal ways." In a 2015 article, he further described the learning ecosystem as a community of people in conjunction with process, information, technology, and their environment. Building on Kelly's article, Robin Lucas, in a 2016 blog post for Fredrickson Learning, suggests it's an internal and external network of people, resources, and technology. I suppose we all see factors that make up ecosystems based on our own experience; if I were to add my two cents' worth, I'd include cognitive attention, because attention and time for learners to process and practice learning is at a premium in our fast-paced world.

Just as there are dangers in the natural ecosystem, as the wildebeest will attest, there are risks within modern organizations. In fact, I often wonder if trainers are endangered species in some organizations because so much is stacked against what they do. Take, for example, the expectations that managers who are uninformed about learning often place on learning departments. A participant from a major global company attending a professional development workshop I facilitated in Denver told me his bosses asked him to cover 10 learning objectives in a one-day workshop. Empirical studies show us that deliberate practice is necessary for learning to happen. How can you fit 10 learning objectives and the necessary practice into a single day? His manager's attitude, which was not informed by the science of learning, was that training existed in a slide deck. To make matters worse, the boss also wanted an extended lunch to celebrate someone's birthday, and they ordered a series of heavy carbohydrates and starches, which made everyone tired in the afternoon.

Is all this depressing? I like to think of it as being helpful. We can become more effective trainers and effect real change in the organizations we serve when we're clear-eyed about the many things stacked against our ability to effectively drive performance. Take, for example, the itty-bitty problem of time. Let's say you're running a class on conflict resolution. You only have the participants for one day because their boss won't give them any more time. "If you're a good teacher," she says condescendingly, "you'll make it work." When you do the math, that one-day workshop represents one day out of, say, 220 workdays a year. That's less than 1 percent of a work year to help them improve their skills. You are such a small element of influence in their performance improvement!

Let's look at it from another angle. Back in the 1980s, the Center for Creative Leadership, in North Carolina, determined that 70 percent of learning about leadership happened on the job, 20 percent through developmental interactions, and 10 percent in the classroom (Biech 2017). Your classroom, webinar, online learning content, or piece of microlearning is just one component in a learning ecosystem that will influence the success of learning. After they watch your inspiring 90-second video or spend a few hours on your awesome webinar, they head back to the workplace, and a bunch of other factors kick in—technology failures, politics, lack of time to practice what they learned. While the 70-20-10 model is not meant to be an exact science and the actual ratio will change depending on the topic you're teaching, it's a helpful model to remind us that our role as trainers, instructional designers, and digital content creators and curators in the learning ecosystem is often tiny.

However, as depressing as this might at first seem, it's actually quite liberating. First, let's take some pressure off ourselves. Second, let's look at how we can influence the other 90 percent of learning. One way is to adjust our mindset and spend less time on being the shiny happy trainer who plans an awesome training experience and start planning activities that support further learning outside the learning event. How can we further help participants take their learning back to the job?

New trainers will spend a lot of time getting their delivery right: "Oh, I followed the curriculum" or "I followed the script." But is that really what it's all about? It's nice to have participants in the safe environment of a conflict-resolution class practice "I statements" and open body language. But will they cut it sitting across the table from a red-faced, angry colleague in a conference room? Will they use or forget the "I statements"? Resilience is as important as content.

Understanding the influence of what happens outside the classroom led me to value the pre-class training conversation. It's a practice considered rudimentary by most trainers: Call the client and run through a series of questions to find out what they need, what their business goals are, what their organizational culture is, and so forth. I'd done a million of these, but now I saw them in a new light. I started to be committed to how the learning would be applied in the workplace and made changes to the curriculum to ensure that it was relevant. But I struggled with this because I realized how little I could really understand each client and the participants' ecosystem. And as a trainer who goes into organizations—I'm not an in-house trainer anymore—how could I ever expect to understand the complexity of organizational needs? Then I remembered another key question. Who builds the learning? Not me. The participant. Rather than find the answers to these questions, I needed to help learners do it. And it starts before we meet in a webinar or classroom and continues well after that.

Long before the term ecosystem came into vogue, a number of thought leaders were talking about the impact of influences outside the training room. Robert Brinkerhoff was one of them. He introduced the High Impact Learning model. He said that training impact happens when planned action related to the business' learning needs happens outside the classroom. In fact, of the learning process, the formal part of instruction—whether it's in the classroom, online, or embedded in some sort of content—accounts for a small part of the learning construction. He suggested that it is improved dramatically when managers have a development conversation with their staff around business needs and learning objectives before they come to class. A follow-up conversation, again focused on business objectives, further improves the impact.

People, Resources, Technology, and Attention

What trainers do in the classroom or during a webinar is simply one element in the overall ecosystem that helps people learn to do their work better. Many more aspects of workplace life outside the learning event will influence them, including other people, on-the-job resources, technology, and their attention.

People

As learning professionals, we can deepen learning by tapping into people outside the classroom who affect a participant's learning and make them part of the learning process. People include their manager, colleagues, support staff, and those outside their organization, such as customers. Studies have shown that manager involvement in learning is critical. Brinkerhoff, as we discussed earlier, talks of the value that managers bring to learning when they engage in a deliberate conversation about learning goals related to the business before and after the class. But there are more people we can consider within the learner's network who might help.

For example, folks with more advanced skill and experience in a topic might provide coaching or mentoring. (The more they mentor or coach others, the more they develop their own expertise, so it's a win-win situation.) If we connect them to fellow learners who can be used to bounce ideas off of, we open another avenue for deliberate retrieval practice and accountability to the topic. And key people outside the organization, who are grounded in the disciplines of topic, could bring a different context and promote a more diverse understanding.

Resources

What resources do learners have to deepen their learning outside the classroom? We're talking about performance support here, something that has long been championed in the human performance improvement field. Trainers can quickly and easily create microlearning content such as job aids, refresher videos, instructional podcasts, or infographics that support learners well after training. (They can also encourage learners to do likewise and share.)

Technology today makes it especially easy for those who may consider themselves artistically challenged. You can use cloud-based infographic programs to design very smart-looking infographics. You can shoot videos on your cell phone and edit them in cheap and cheerful software programs. There's no end to the support you can create: self-reflection checklists, workflow summaries, cheat sheets, buzzword guides, and the like. But many resources you don't even need to create. More and more trainers are adding content curation to their content-creation skills. There's no need to reinvent the wheel when excellent resources are available for free as well as for purchase or subscription. And then there are the resources your learners share. Some of the best teaching resources I use today have been taught to me by participants who have found a key video or shared an exercise that better highlights something I've taught. How can you get them sharing these with one another?

Technology

Whenever you talk about the new world of learning, the conversation inadvertently turns to technology. Many organizations extend learning using learning management systems or content sharing platforms. There's a very long list of companies who would be willing to see you use their system for tracking learners and delivering just-in-time content. Now artificial intelligence is coming into the mix and being used to help predict learner needs, delivering it in a way that supports learning. In addition, robots will soon have a role to play as they become more sophisticated. Robots are already writing news stories for some of the world's leading newspapers. How can you leverage artificial intelligence in your organization? You may need to hire a specialist, but it won't be long before programs and apps do the heavy lifting when designing how to gather the data you need, making it easy to apply.

There has been a lot of buzz around mobile learning over the past five years. This makes content available on phones and tablets so learners can learn anywhere at anytime. How can you leverage the fabulous opportunity to have refresher content available to someone when they need it? It's more than thinking about putting content on a phone and involves thinking about how you can predict need and ensure the right element of learning is packaged in the right way at the right time. Next is embedding learning into everyday objects.

Attention

We've talked a lot already about the need for learners to have time and space to process and practice what they learn. A single learning event or piece of content cannot guarantee learning, especially with complex topics. The expectation that it might—when it is one day in 220—is probably unreasonable, unless it's incredibly designed and allows time after the event for the learner to engage in deliberate practice. But how often is practice given the time it needs? As you plan learning, think about what you might do to reinforce the need for learners to practice their new skills beyond the classroom. Can you petition managers to have their staff take time out for deliberate practice? Can you do follow-up coaching to ask questions that promote retrieval? Can you influence leaders to instill a culture in which learning is seen as a long-term commitment, not a copy and paste activity? Better still, can you help learners learn how to learn—the art of metacognition?

The Mindset

Learning happens in the learner's brain. Anywhere the learner is—in or outside the virtual or physical classroom—learning can happen, at any time. It's so easy to focus lots of energy into crafting the perfect classroom or virtual learning experience and forget that learners leave that experience and are immediately influenced by the people around them, the resources they have to retain the learning, the technology they can access it on, and the time they have to give attention to practice. So many things interact and can reinforce or hinder what you helped them learn, just like simple things such as disease can change the food chain in the Maasai Mara. It's so complex that we really can't begin to do justice to it with a description.

I used to plan workshops based on the classroom experience because the outlook in the training world was that what we did in the classroom was the important thing. Such a mindset was comfortable because it was tangible, easy to conceptualize, and easy to predict. It was also unrealistic because learning isn't restricted to the vacuum of a classroom. The only way to be successful was to see learning as something that extended way before and after the classroom, when we interacted with learners. To be successful, I needed to tap into what happened beyond the classroom. But things often work against us—especially when if, like me, you are not part of an organization. It does take adopting a mindset, like I have, where we ask some simple questions all based on how we could affect people's learning so it extended beyond the classroom. Here are the questions I ask:

- Who in the workplace will affect the success of learning? Can I or the learner identify and leverage their influence?
- What resources can I find to support learning after the classroom? How can I make them truly relevant for the learner?
- What technologies can I use to support the application of learning on the job? Am I thinking about the latest technologies that are making learning more agile?
- What can I do to ensure that learners carve out space to engage in deliberate practice? Whom do I need to talk to make this happen and hold learners accountable to practice?

After three days, I was able to leave my tent and experience the dynamics of the Maasai Mara. I was still feeling slightly ill, but the feelings in my stomach quickly gave way to feelings of awe as I saw giraffe, lions, elephants, and even a rare white rhino in their natural habitat, each playing its influential part in balancing the ecosystem. Every action one animal took had a knock-on effect, affecting other animals whether they be the same breed or higher or lower in the food chain. Seeing this helped me reflect on the fact that we too experience a set of dynamics in the workplace, not unlike the Mara or other natural environments like rainforests.

I bet you can think of many elements beyond the classroom that affect whether what you did in class is successful. People and their behavior—supervisors, colleagues, and customers. Technology to support learning—platforms, their reach, and their reliability. The time learners have for practice to truly embed the learning. To be really smart, we need to design classroom strategies to extend the pedagogy beyond the classroom so it deliberately influences these other elements.

8

TRAINING DOESN'T SUCK, BUT THEY DON'T KNOW THAT

If history were taught in the form of stories, it would never be forgotten.
—Rudyard Kipling

SHE WAS TALL, ELEGANT, AND TANNED, wearing what looked like a Cartier watch on her wrist. With large, dark sunglasses, she was dressed in a white linen suit and pastel-blue shirt with an oversized collar. He was in linens, too, and standing nearby. A white suit as well, but a crisply starched black shirt, open at the top. Both stood steady as a rock, unaffected by the gentle rocking of the 80-foot motor yacht. He clutched a Moleskine in his right hand, with what looked like an expensive Mont Blanc pen in his left, as she talked to someone on her phone. She was the boss, the owner of a sprawling multinational company that had holdings in multiple industries. He was her personal assistant.

Known for his discretion and ruthless attention to detail, he accompanied her everywhere as she called the shots across her vast empire.

This was Monte Carlo, July 2009. The Tour de France was about to start, and my wife and I sat on the balcony of our hotel, overlooking the marina.

Quite frankly, we had no idea who these people were. Or the older couple sipping something out of liquor glasses on the boat berthed next to theirs. We were just making it all up. It's a game we sometimes play—crafting stories about people—to boost our "imagination quotient." There aren't too many rules: We must be respectful. And because we take turns, we build on the story so far; we can't change facts that have already been established. We look at people, context, what they're wearing, how they walk, how they interact, and what they're doing. Sometimes we imagine they're international spies, at other times reluctant millionaires. It doesn't really matter what shape the story takes; it's just a lot of fun, especially when accompanied, as it was on this occasion, by a bottle of Moët & Chandon.

I'd been facilitating a leadership workshop in the South of France and my wife had joined me, so we stayed the weekend to "do Monte Carlo." The plan was to visit the casino that night, because that's where James Bond had had some fun. But we were tired, and it was so miserably hot that we just couldn't be bothered to dress up and walk past the cycling festivities to the casino. The story exercise was the perfect alternative.

But did you know everyone does this without thinking? We make stories up whenever someone walks into the office. He's dressed in a suit, so he must be management. She drives a BMW, so she must make a lot of money. Human beings need stories for survival. They help us make sense of the world, which gives us a feeling of control and order. That's why we buy newspapers, read blog posts, and share gossip around the watercooler. Even if you're not sitting on that balcony in Monte Carlo overlooking the marina and playing the story game, you're processing what you see, hear, feel, smell, and taste to build mental models that explain what's going on.

Every person who comes into your training class has a story about you based on contact they may have had before the class started, how you walk, speak, and interact with them. Or what they read about you on the Internet. Or something they heard about you or the class from a previous participant.

I recall a conversation from a conference while I stood in line between sessions. Two people in front of me were commiserating about attending a training class, convinced it was a waste of time. They had heard a negative story about the training from a colleague. That story was influencing their expectations of this class, before they even had a chance to experience it. Unfortunately, this is not uncommon. Around the world, there are people who dislike what their training department does because they've heard a story or two about training having been poorly delivered or simply designed without being aligned to needs. Sometimes these impressions are valid but very often they're not, and they make it harder for us to demonstrate the value we offer an organization and motivate learners to engage. It stinks, because most workplace trainers I know are passionate about their work and invest considerable time and energy to make their programs really count. In fact, many go above and beyond, putting in overtime and enduring travel schedules that cut into their weekends and family time.

I've heard disparaging remarks made about training all around the world. Sometimes it's to my face; at other times, it's through passive aggressive comments like, "Isn't the training department where they send workers who aren't any good at their job?" Or, knowing you're within earshot, they mutter that tired old line, "If you can't do, you teach." (Personally, I like the next line, "If you can't teach, you teach gym.") Sometimes, this lack of respect for training is expressed in the form of low participation rates or people turning up late and not engaging in class activities. Whatever the reasons, the stories have impact.

Why People Don't Like Training

Some of these reasons are easy to understand. A bad classroom or webinar experience can easily cloud someone's view: an unprepared trainer, or ad hoc delivery. Participants treated poorly or with disrespect. A room that was too hot or cold. A webinar platform that crashed every time a video was shared. Outdated curriculums and job aids. While a skillful trainer might prevent many of these issues from occurring, once the damage has been done, it can take longer to restore a reputation.

Another common cause is that managers outside training or talent development are clueless about what the department does. They don't understand that our purpose is to help their staff work better. They are fixed in a traditional mindset where they see training as an event they send staff to so they can hear someone read PowerPoint slides to them.

Negative stories about training are not good. They affect people's motivation to participate. They affect whether managers engage us when they have a problem, rather than at the last moment, when they have no alternative. They also affect what budgeters think. Remember the accountant who called me wanting an elastic workforce? His story of trainers is that the only time they did any work was when they were in the classroom. He had no idea that preparation and coaching after class took place. And because of that, he was ready to recommend culling the department.

We need to flip this perception. Managers and their teams need to know that workplace learning can help them learn new skills and deepen existing ones. They need to know that we can help them work more easily. Speed up the time it takes to complete tasks. Improve quality. And ultimately get them a raise.

So what do we do? We need to educate people in our organizations about how we can help them. And evangelize to managers and their teams the value that talent professionals bring to their work.

Scroll Down, Man!

About 15 years ago, the executive producer of a popular program that was broadcast weekly sent me an email. The first line read, "Jonathan, I sent some writers to your writing workshop. I asked them how it helped. See below."

Oh, crap, I could see what was coming. Some rants about how the workshop was ineffective. Have you ever received one of those emails? You sit there debating whether you should scroll down and read what you assume is going to be negative feedback. Don't we always expect the worse? So instead of reading on, I went to the restroom. Then, I stopped in the kitchen for a coffee and idle conversation with a colleague who was microwaving her lunch. Then, when I couldn't find any other distractions, I returned to my desk. "Hit me," I said out loud.

A colleague at another desk looked my way. "Huh?"

"Oh, nothing," I mumbled. But then, as I scrolled, I smiled.

"As a result of Jonathan's workshop, I have much more confidence writing. And in fact, I'm saving on average between 60 and 90 minutes every day because he taught some techniques to speed up my writing." *Wow,* I thought to myself. I scratched on the back of an envelope what that would mean over a year. If she saved just one hour every day, she's saved five hours a week. Twenty hours a month. Adding it all up, she'd save six weeks. Now, life isn't as clean-cut as that. There are variables. But now she was writing better for her program and freeing her time up for more creativity, more writing, or more time in the coffee shop. It's amazing.

Just like you've probably received emails complaining about your training, you are likely to have stories like this that you could share—probably more impressive ones, too. Think for a moment about how that little story shows the value of the executive producer's training investment. A day out of the office actually made up for itself within two weeks. The executive producer saved some money and was able to broadcast more and better content by investing in a simple one-day class. And in the executive producer's head is the story, "I send staff to training—and it speeds up production," rather than, "Geez, she's out of the office for a whole day. I have to wait for her to come back to finish this project."

And future learning candidates? They won't be thinking, "I bet that trainer will just ramble on and on forever and I'll be bored to tears" but rather, "This could save me five hours a week; I want to do some more training." I can't help but think that positive stories make people want to come to class to learn. And make managers want to support their staff by paying for their training.

But the problem is that most managers, as well as the staff who have to attend our classes, have other stories in their heads. And like the stories my wife and I made up in Monte Carlo, I can't help but wonder if many of their stories about training being a bore or a waste of time are fiction, based on assumptions that have little basis in fact. But how can we expect anything else, given that they don't know the good stories? I think we can do better. Trainers need to be ambassadors and tell people all the ways we help folks.

Ambassador for Talent

If I were to go back into the corporate world and take a chief learning officer or training director gig, I'd rewrite every one of my trainers' job descriptions to include the skill of educating stakeholders and potential stakeholders on how talent professionals help organizations work better and the value they bring.

When I was a learning executive, it was natural for people like me to do most of this. My teams worked at the coalface, delivering 40 to 50 excellent workshops every week, while I went to meetings, met with managers, and spoke at internal conferences about how good my folks were. (And by the way, they were very good. I'm not just saying this; to this day, their work still inspires me.) But today, in an age when stories travel faster than facts, simply having the boss do this work is not enough. I think every trainer needs to be blowing the trumpet of training. We need to be ambassadors for talent.

INSIDER TIP

So many people write books about communication. Which is best? *Made to Stick* by Chip and Dan Heath is my favorite from the last decade. It models what it teaches and, in particular, offers a very practical chapter on how to structure stories to influence people. Important note: This is a different book to *Make It Stick*.

This means telling stories about how training has helped the organization or individuals. Why stories? Not only do they help people make sense of things, they are easy to remember. During my teen years, my brother and I would spend summers with our step grandmother. We'd travel from Sydney to Adelaide and learn about writing from her. You see, she was a novelist; under the pseudonym Charlotte Jay, she won the first Edgar Allen Poe Award in 1954 for a book she set in Papua New Guinea. Another of her books, *The Fugitive Eye,* was made into a telemovie starring Charlton Heston for ABC TV's *The Alcoa Hour,* introduced by Fred Astaire. We adored her because she was so matter of fact but also because she treated us like adults—and asked us for our opinions on things from science to religion. We'd sit with her for hours, as she held a cigarette in one hand and a gin and tonic in the other, talking about stories.

With 15 books, translated into multiple languages, she taught me a lot. But one thing that stuck out was that people remember stories. Tell a good story and people will remember and share it; the more they share it, the more they remember it. People don't remember facts. For example, they don't remember that your average Level 1 evaluation score is 4.4. They remember that you helped them change the way they work—sell more products, for example, which led to better commissions. I think trainers understand this. Most have seen how people in their classes forget facts. But when you tell them a story, they remember the story, and the facts come easier.

Our Stories

If we're going to tell stories about how training has transformed an organization or helped people do better work, where do you get them? And how do you back them up? One place is your training department's evaluation team. In midsized to large training organizations, there's usually one or more folks dedicated to evaluating the effectiveness of learning. Go talk to them about where the results are, then go and find stories that explain the figures.

Formal evaluation studies are not the only place to go for great stories to educate and evangelize stakeholders on the value of training. We've all got many stories like the one I received in my inbox. These are the sorts of things you need to be shouting about out loud. But it isn't always easy, because it can feel a little like bragging too much. I now share the story about the email regularly, but it took a lot of courage because I didn't want to seem boastful.

If you're not comfortable talking about your stories, why not get stories from your colleagues and rave about their work? Share your success stories in exchange, and let them rave about yours. If you manage or lead the learning function in your company, why not schedule a 90-minute meeting every month for your trainers to share their success stories? Discuss their stories, and then get them to talk one another up. I wished I'd done that back when I was leading Production Training at the BBC.

Making Stories Work for You

It's up to you how formally you want to use stories and results to educate people on the value of learning. But there are a number of things worth considering.

The first is to be careful about what stories you tell. You want to be sure that these stories show the impact of learning and how it helps the business. A mistake I often see is trainers talking about the learning experience. They'll talk about how the program is interactive and involves multimedia content. But what manager cares about whether it's interactive or a great learning experience? They're more interested in knowing what people are doing after the event and how it links to improving the business.

Consider the time I rolled out training for 600 journalists at a major newspaper. No one wanted to attend because they were in the middle of a significant change initiative, moving from the paper and ink world into the digital age. Many were frightened about the new technology—they were phenomenal writers, but making video was a bridge too far. We found that after the first two weeks, after journalists went back to the newsroom and started making decent videos, other journalists started wanting to come to the training. They weren't interested in the training because someone said, "They're using neuro-linguistic programming techniques to teach it." They were interested because they knew they would most likely have the skills for basic video after attending.

When you tell success stories, share them in terms of what participants gained and how their new skills contributed to the organization's goals.

Second, think about whom you are telling the story to. I learned this from Theresa Seagraves, author of the book *Quick! Show Me Your Value* (2004). Different people at different levels of the organization speak different corporate languages. For example, a trainer may see a workshop as being successful because everything flowed smoothly and the class got through the content. However, the chief financial officer probably doesn't care much about whether the session went smoothly. She's more interested in whether the training session led to a return on investment. Speaking the language of executives is critical; however, very few people in training departments have these skills. I guess this is because few were formerly CEOs or executive vice presidents. Most trainers come to the learning department from functional roles such as mechanic, accountant, supervisor, or salesperson. So speaking like the folks in the C-suite can present a steep learning curve.

INSIDER TIP

It's not easy to convince senior leaders about the value of training. Often, it's because we don't talk their language. In *Quick! Show Me Your Value*, Theresa Seagraves offers practical tips in this easy-to-read book on how to influence the folks who make financial decisions about training.

Being able to tell our stories to different audiences is important because while we need to communicate the link between training and bottom-line results to executives, we also need to communicate different things to people who perform the roles. This could include ensuring that salespeople can see that this workshop will help them close more deals, or helping workers in a factory see that training can reduce the number of workplace accidents.

Third, we need to be strategic with our stories. Any marketer will tell you that it's critical to have a consistent message that supports a product's or service's sales. If you have different messages, you lose that strong, focused impact. We need to be clear about the messages we are sending to the organization about how learning can help. This links into branding and positioning. What do you want people to think of your talent department and the work it does? When you share these stories, ask how they promote this brand. For example, if you're trying to educate people about the value of coaching, find a way in your story to show how coaching improved results.

Who Tells the Story?

One of the fascinating changes to take place in my lifetime is the media revolution. In newspapers, TV, and radio, we went from a broadcast mentality to a conversational mindset. Fifteen years ago, a newspaper columnist would write a 400-word comment. If anyone wanted to challenge or add to her words, they had a shot at the Letters to the Editor page, which printed about eight of the hundreds and sometimes thousands of letters a newspaper would receive each day. But today, anyone can write a comment on the columnist's ideas by simply signing up and adding to the narrative.

You might be thinking after reading this last chapter that everything I said fits into the old way of communicating. Telling our own stories of success is one thing, similar to a corporate brand shooting off a public relations piece about its volunteer efforts or environmental stewardship. With so much information out in the world now, it's too easy for that message to get lost. To really have impact, we need to get other people telling our stories. The more the stakeholders are aware of the training successes, involved in them, and excited by them, the more we can ask them to share the successes of training. If a computer implementation happened without a hitch because the training was well organized, then get these folks talking about it and sing the praises of their involvement. It's valuable social credibility.

Brands understand that the key to success is to unlock a grassroots movement around promotion and storytelling; trainers can learn a lot from that playbook. It's what happened at the newspaper company with 600 journalists. Not only were print journalists making videos that looked good, they were talking about how the workshop equipped them to do so, generating interest among other journalists to complete the training.

Training Doesn't Suck—Well, Most of It, Anyway

Our profession faces some perception challenges about what we do and the value we bring to an organization. I know this is not a problem in every organization, but it is in many. And I wonder if it's because folks form ideas in their heads about training in much the same way my wife and I played that story game in Monte Carlo. While the employees in your organization might be basing this off a valid experience, that's not the complete story of training—only part of it. We need to give stakeholders real stuff to build stories that promote how we can help them and motivate them to use training. We need to be strategically sharing stories of training's success.

Now, there is still training that does genuinely suck: Poorly prepared trainers. Workshops not aligned to business objectives. Trainers still locked to PowerPoint slides like an umbilical cord. There's no point in telling stories about that; we simply need to do better and get the training right. Because if we don't share the stories of how training does help people and organizations, they will make it up themselves. And they probably won't tell the stories we need them to tell.

A Trainer Disarms a Disruptive Participant

Wesley E. Anderson

FOR A RECENT GIG, I was brought in to work with a group of senior staff to improve their clinical documentation and services. I had done my research beforehand both on the regulations that govern their work and on their internal processes. The day was going smoothly, with meaningful participation from everyone in the room. Well, everyone but one.

Throughout the morning Bob, a member of the senior staff, had all but refused to engage in activities or discussions. Bob was a master of that combative, yet subtle, hostility that teachers and trainers know well. He rolled his eyes. He sighed loudly. He texted and argued. What's worse, Bob was influential. Like the Fourth Horseman of the Trainer Apocalypse, Bob's actions heralded the eventual death of the workshop. The typical advice for "dealing with a disruptive participant" made no difference.

Finally, during a debrief after a group activity it was Bob's turn to share his ideas for program improvement. He looked me in the eye and with the smallest of smirks said, "Cut down on pointless trainings."

The room went silent. It was clear to everyone that Bob was looking for a fight and my impulse was to give him one. Instead, I let the silence linger for a moment before calmly asking, "Bob, what's the last pointless training you had to participate in?"

All eyes turned back to Bob, who turned bright red before saying, "I . . . I can't think of one off the top of my head."

Just like that you could almost see Bob's ability and desire to negatively influence the room deflate. He began participating and apologized to me after the training. I realized that maintaining the illusion of the trainer that is oblivious to passive aggressive disruptions sometimes dehumanizes us and is ultimately counterproductive. Bob wanted to fight with the trainer persona in front of him, but I didn't give him the option. Instead, I all but dared him to cross the line of professionalism and he chose to step back.

We can't avoid the Bobs of the world, but we can hold a mirror up and ask them, "Is this who you want to be?"

Wesley Anderson is the director of training and consultation services at The Arc of New Jersey.

9

GRAB THE OXYGEN MASK: SUSTAINING YOUR MOJO

Ninety percent of life is keeping calm.
—Dr. Chris Feudtner

TRAINERS ARE EXPECTED to be perfect people professionals, and we certainly are not supposed to admit that people sometimes annoy us. We're supposed to smile and look like everyone makes us happy, right? Fake it till you make it—or something like that. We wouldn't want that negative feedback.

And yet, on a Friday after lunch, in 2014, I insulted someone in North Carolina. It wasn't United's gate agent, who announced that my flight was late. Or the cab driver, who got lost, making me later. No, it was a participant in my workshop. My insult wasn't terrible. She simply asked a question about instructions I'd given for an exercise, instructions I'd already repeated three times for other participants who had been having side conversations. So, I answered, "Well, as I've said three times . . ." While that reads nicer on paper, with my tone of voice, it came out dripping with snark. Except—she hadn't been one of the people talking. Uh oh. Afterward, she felt so offended that she wrote on her evaluation form, "Other participants were talking, and I couldn't hear the instructions. He was rude and seemed indignant I wanted to learn." Her comment, written with a ballpoint pen, left an indentation in the paper.

As a learning professional, I don't like to operate or respond with derisiveness, no matter how difficult an individual or group is. I genuinely like people, and I see it as my duty to help foster a safe environment where they can focus on the hard work of learning. But there was a reason for my snarky reaction, albeit not an excuse. I had just experienced a grueling week by anyone's standards. It started with me finishing up a three-day program in Irvine, California, on Wednesday. That night, I caught a red eye to Washington. While I slept on the first leg to Denver, I sat next to a loud snorer on the second flight and couldn't get comfortable. Stumbling off the plane right after 8 a.m. on Thursday, I had six hours to go home, jump on a 90-minute business call, and head back to the airport, meanwhile finding time to fit in basic necessities like hygiene and food, all before my flight to Charlotte. Arriving early in the evening, I crashed on the bed for a fourth night on the road, tossing and turning. Up at 5 a.m. to ready myself for a day of facilitating, I knocked back the thickest coffee I could find. I was bone tired. Despite all that, I still should have been more dignified responding to her question. But at this point, I felt like I was running low on my training mojo.

Many trainers live in a state of chronic exhaustion. Increased workloads are the new normal in most organizations. We're on the road much more, bouncing from corporate office to corporate office. And rather than leave work at work, we bring it home and access email almost 24/7, cutting into our sleep time and ramping up our stress levels. According to Gallup, 40 percent of adults get fewer than six hours of sleep a night, and sleep experts tell us adults need seven to nine hours (Jones 2013). The *Huffington Post* reports that stress is responsible for 75 to 95 percent of visits to the doctor (Robinson 2013). No wonder society is seeing higher rates of heart disease, diabetes, stroke, obesity, asthma, depression, headaches, gastrointestinal conditions, premature aging, and more.

What's Holding Us Back?

Hari Sutha Raj runs Daksada, a talent development company in Dubai that helps leaders improve morale and performance. The company's Transform 360 is a leadership program that stakes part of its success on promoting the personal well-being of the leader. In fact, before the program starts, participants undertake a physical before learning how to develop energy and stamina for optimal performance. I asked Hari what challenges he thought trainers face in this high-stress world. "Trainers are on their feet all day and are prone to sprains and tension, especially in the shoulders and lower back," he said. And he suggested that trainers need to be physically fit and have a healthy mind. How often do we hear about being physically fit and having a healthy mind in train-the-trainer programs?

But it makes sense. Effective facilitators need a certain mojo to maintain good people skills from early in the morning until late in the afternoon. This includes the mental agility to stay focused and keep learners' attention on the learning. The stamina to respond to the emotional and logistic needs of learners. And the physical energy to stay on their feet all day. Not to mention being cheerful and responsive to learners' needs when they ask for help during your lunch break or hang around after class with questions when you're dying to go home. Whether it's a poor diet because you're on the road, not enough sleep because you're stressed, demanding clients, or a heavy workload, it seems as if the odds are stacked against maintaining this mojo.

Diet

I don't think you need to be a nutrition expert to know that diet is critical to maintaining energy levels. Numerous studies show that certain foods aid the brain, such as fish and nuts, while other foods actually inhibit brain function. Some foods take the brain on an energy roller-coaster ride—yes, we're talking about sugar. As a general rule, fresh food translates into nutrition and energy to fuel the body. But how often do you have access to fresh food? If you travel a lot from your home base, there's a good chance you're skipping meals, having them at the wrong time of the day, or eating heavily processed food that lacks nutrients. Even if you eat in nice restaurants, the food isn't guaranteed to be fresh. And forget about food served on planes and in hotel bars.

Sleep

A Harvard study suggested lack of sleep cost business $63 billion in lost productivity (Kessler 2011). The practical result is that lack of sleep slows down reaction time and hinders the brain's ability to form solid memories. According to the National Sleep Foundation (n.d.), sleeplessness makes it harder to pay attention. More alarmingly, chronic lack of sleep is equivalent to being drunk. Charles A. Czeisler, a sleep specialist interviewed in the *Harvard Business Review,* says that people who average just four hours of sleep for four or five days in a row develop the same level of cognitive impairment they'd have if they had been awake for 24 hours, equivalent to a 0.1 percent blood alcohol level, which is considered legally drunk (Fryer 2006). We wouldn't allow a trainer to show up to class inebriated, but how many live on four or five hours' sleep?

Sleep is tough for a lot of people, especially when under stress (up next). One reason is that things just seem worse at night. I call it midnight madness. I wake up in a cold sweat worrying that my equipment will fail in the classroom the next day, or that I've packed the wrong workbooks. When this happens, I just use self-talk and say, "This is midnight madness." After a while, it goes away. The other pressure is lying in bed and not falling asleep. For many people, it makes things worse because they look at the clock at 3 a.m. and think, "I only have two hours left to fall asleep!" Then at 4 a.m., "I only have one hour . . ."

Stress

A few weeks ago, I was joking with a friend who lives in the Washington, D.C., area, where I live, that the city fuels itself on cortisol. Cortisol is the stress drug that causes inflammation and can lead to higher triglyceride levels. So many people we know complain about being stressed—and I'm one of them. According to HeartMath (2014), the ability to concentrate and remember has a lot to do with how much emotional stress we're experiencing. And stress, whether it be a house move, new job, knowing someone said something nasty about you, or simply needing to meet a deadline, has a dramatic effect on cognitive function.

A lot of things in a trainer's life can lead to stress. Not because they are necessarily bad things; it's just the way things are. People are late to class, and you need to get them up to speed. The temperature control in a room isn't working, and you have to find a way to stop participants from freezing. The desks are arranged in the wrong way, and you have to change them quickly before participants arrive. The data projector doesn't work with your laptop, even though it did yesterday. You run an exercise, and it doesn't go the way you expected.

Lack of Personal Time

Diet, sleep, and stress aren't the only factors that affect a trainer's well-being. If you're an introvert and spend seven hours in a class-room, plus an hour before and after setting up and prepping for the following day, you'll finish the day exhausted. The introversion versus extroversion theory was first put forward in the early 20th century by Carl Jung, the German psychotherapist. Unlike the popular idea that introverts are just quiet people and extroverts are noisy, Jung suggested that introverts draw their energy from within, while extroverts get their energy from outside.

At the risk of being simplistic, the difference looks like this. To recharge their batteries, introverts at the end of the day's training will withdraw to their hotel and not talk to anyone. They'll emerge the following day with all the energy they need. Extroverts, however, need to be with people. To recharge, they prefer dinner with colleagues or hanging out in the bar, where they can talk with other folks. Recent studies suggest that the difference is caused by blood flow to the brain—introverts have stronger flow, which provides stimulation, while extroverts have less. An introvert sitting in a busy restaurant will be overwhelmed by the sensory stimuli of music, chatting, clattering plates, and echoing conversations. In contrast, an extrovert will be stim-ulated by these things.

Trainers are constantly interacting with people, and if they are introverted, this causes considerable stress. They need time out to recharge their batteries and often don't get it.

Demanding Clients

We love our clients, right? Ah. I had a client who used to phone me at 10 at night. Both my wife and I are introverts. We love hanging out with friends, but on a weeknight, as we get older, we increasingly like to batten down the hatches at 7 p.m. So, this client, as much as I enjoyed serving his company, was a pain in the derriere. It posed a problem: Am I being rude if I don't take the call?

Bridget, who is a one-person training department in a small manufacturing company in the Midwest, told me that she has internal clients who will request changes to her programs the night before she delivers them. She's found herself staying late, missing her son's soccer games, changing participant guides, and hitting the photocopier. "Should I just say I'm not changing anything and risk damaging their perception of what we bring to the organization?" she asked me.

She's not alone. If you're an external trainer, it might be a client's systems that cause stress. One client I thought the world of needed me to interact with their SAP software system, which was ideal for multinationals but not small companies with one or two trainers. Then you have financial stresses, like the clients who require that you book your travel a month in advance, but then won't pay for 90 days while it sits on your credit card, costing you interest and stopping your access to cash. If you're an internal trainer, you might experience Bridget's situation—the client who asks you to change something in the program the night before, or the manager who promises information about the business a week before class, but gets it to you the day before the presentation.

Jetlag

If you're traveling across time zones, your body probably feels as if it's never quite ahead. Studies show that jetlag can, in the long term, affect memory and learning as well as impede reaction times. It's also been shown to contribute to conditions such as diabetes, heart disease, hypertension, and cancer. Most of us feel the immediate effects, though: not being able to sleep when you should and struggling to stay awake when you need to. Add into the bargain the dehydration from the pressurized aircraft cabins, and many people also suffer from constipation or diarrhea. Yeah, they didn't tell you that when you started traveling. The body craves routine and homeostasis, and traveling across time zones actively wars against this need.

Workload

How often have you heard people talk about working 80-hour weeks? How often have you heard folks suggesting that their office couldn't survive without them? A lot of people wear these long weeks as a badge of honor, although to me it's actually a badge of dishonor. Their office probably desperately needs them to take a little time off, even if their bosses don't realize it.

Long hours are generally bad for your health. Studies show that long working hours has a significant impact on workers, increasing the risk of hypertension, cardiovascular disease, fatigue, stress, depression, muscular skeletal disorders, and chronic infections. Toronto's Institute for Work and Health found that women had a 63 percent higher chance of diabetes over a 12-year period when working 45 or more hours a week, compared with women working 35 to 40 hours (Gilbert-Ouimet et al. 2018). According to WebMD, a study across Denmark, Sweden, Finland, and the United Kingdom showed that people putting in 55 hours or more, compared with the traditional 35 to 40 hours a week, had a 1.4 times higher risk of developing irregular heartbeats, or atrial fibrillation (Kivimäki et al. 2017). And other studies have shown that working more than 55 hours a week over seven years increased the odds of a stroke by 33 percent and heart disease by 13 percent (Kivimäki et al. 2015).

If you're sick or suffering from a chronic health condition because you've been working long hours, you can't perform up to your usual productivity levels. Studies have shown that the longer you work, the less productive you are and the more mistakes you make. While a quick nap can help bring performance back, we simply are not as effective at the end of a 12-hour day.

I've quoted a bunch of studies about the risks in working long hours. However, I'd be remiss if I didn't also say that a small number of studies have found that in some cases, the long hours are not as bad as we first thought. But this is only when the person loves doing the work. When you are passionate about something you are doing, perhaps when you're in a creative flow, it seems that you are less likely to become stressed in the same way. In a nutshell, if you love your work, you won't be battling all the negative side effects. This is good news until you consider how much you might not love your work.

Multitasking

Despite years of people touting their ability to do two, three, or four things at once, the trend seems to be reversing, with more and more people knowing that the notion of multitasking is a myth. The science tells us that it's physiologically not possible. We may sometimes think we are multitasking, but in reality, we're jumping back and forth between tasks. We transition so quickly that it feels like we're doing three things at once but we really aren't. So what's the problem? Studies have shown that multitaskers are actually up to 40 percent less productive than those who focus on one task at a time (Mautz 2017). This is because switching from one task to another requires considerable cognitive resources. It also has implications for how we work and the interruptions we experience when sitting at our desks each day. According to *Fast Company*, it takes an average of 23 minutes and 15 seconds to get back to a task that was interrupted (Pattison 2008). What does this mean when we're at our desks and an email comes while we're in the middle of planning something or writing an article? It means that we've severely disrupted our train of thought, and getting back to that state of creativity will require additional time.

Secure Your Oxygen Mask First

When I think about all the items I've discussed that are holding us back, I'm not surprised. If I'm honest, it's kind of obvious that less sleep stops us from performing at our peak and can undermine our ability to do good work. It's not difficult to recognize that poor diet leads to fatigue, further stress, and physical ailments such as obesity, diabetes, and heart disease, each of which makes us more sluggish and exerts more stress on our life. That high workload makes us grumpy. And kidding ourselves that we are multitasking just slows us down.

When I chat about this to other trainers, they nod their heads, and then none of us does anything. Too many people in our profession are running on fumes. It's easy to descend the slow, winding road to burnout, stacking training engagements up against one another and not allowing for time to pause and reflect. This is ridiculous. Facilitating learning is intensive—you are "on" from 7:30 a.m. until 5:30 p.m., with people watching your every move while you think through what they're doing and how to help them do it well. It's not the same as sitting in an office, where you can take a break, walk to the watercooler, or go hide in a meeting and say nothing.

That's why I now have an oxygen strategy. Every time you take off in an airplane, the crew runs through the safety demonstration (more on travel in the next chapter). It's been a long time since I've mindfully watched one, but as I recall, they advise that in the "unlikely event" that the cabin loses pressure, oxygen masks will fall from the overhead compartment. Their instruction is to put your mask on first. If you're sitting next to a child or an elderly person, don't do their mask first. Put on yours first, because then you'll have the oxygen and be alive to help them.

It's the same for trainers. If we don't look after ourselves, we won't have the mental acuity to really support learners in the work of learning through real feedback, encouragement, and practice. Instead, we'll snap at unsuspecting participants, like that poor woman in North Carolina.

So what do we do about it? Hari Sutha Raj suggests three areas in his work with executives. First, he says, develop routines because they free your mind to focus your energy on creative pursuits. Second, be clear on your objectives—he's a big fan of SMART objectives. Third, adopt activities such as yoga to decompress and energize the body. What do these things look like for the workplace trainer? Building on Hari's thoughts, I think it involves things such as setting clear boundaries, committing to strategies that help you decompress, increasing physical activities, and managing your personal energy.

INSIDER TIP

It's easy to think we can relieve stress by being better time-managers. But Jim Loehr and Tony Schwartz suggest in their book *The Power of Full Engagement* that it's about managing your energy. Grab this book for scientifically grounded, practical tips on managing energy, which is critical for high performance.

Set Boundaries

Ever had a client call or text you late at night, when you're winding down for the evening? It's easy to think it's rude not to take their call. Has a supervisor asked you to make a massive change to a program you spent two weeks planning at 5 p.m. the day before it rolls out? It's easy to think you're inflexible if you don't drop the planning and wing it. The IT department calls three weeks before a big technology rollout asking your team to train 2,000 staff members, something they should have planned months ago. It's an impossible situation that training departments find themselves in far too often.

These scenarios are common, and sometimes we have no choice. More often, though, we have more control than we think and need to say no. But how do you know what to say no to? Bestselling author Jim Collins has spoken at a number of ATD's international conferences, and I was inspired when he said that successful people don't have a to-do list. They have a not-to-do list. Successful people know what not to do and when to say no. However, many of us, for one reason or another, are slaves to our to-do list, which just makes us feel guilty when we can't complete it. Knowing what not to do is about setting boundaries. This is not a book on boundaries—developing them takes wisdom, self-awareness, strength, and conflict-resolution skills. What's important to keep in mind is that very often we make decisions based on what we think others will think of us, rather than what makes sense for the situation. And often, we fail to give ourselves the permission to educate others on what's reasonable and not.

To set effective boundaries, we need to be clear on our priorities and develop the skill to articulate how our boundaries achieve those priorities. Some of the boundaries I have set are the result of seeing a coach. Workload is an area where having boundaries is especially important if we're to avoid stretching ourselves too thin and be committed to delivering top-quality work. We've already discussed the cost of working more than 45 hours a week on productivity and health. But how many folks do you meet who admit to putting in more than 50 hours a week? I know I do; I've lost track of how many weekends I've worked and how many times I've taken work home, pushing aside time that should have been used for relaxing and recharging my batteries. I like to excuse this overwork by implying that I'm in demand, but when I think through why I'm working weekends, it's usually because I overcommit to things and make poor planning decisions, or forget to add travel time to bookings and then run classes too close to one another. Being able to say no is about boundaries, which takes confidence but prevents me from underperforming. The confidence to establish boundaries takes time to develop, but it's worth it.

Another boundary issue relates to agreeing to what we deliver. Many clients have unrealistic expectations. For example, they think that a half-day presentation is all staff will need to learn how to manage conflict. Wrong. They need deliberate practice backed up and supported throughout the learning ecosystem. We need to educate clients on what is possible and what is not. If you're a corporate in-house trainer, it's helpful to develop a client service agreement that sets these things out. It should cover timelines for development, what happens when things go off plan, and who is responsible for different aspects of the training.

It's also important to set boundaries between you and participants. We're not psychologists who need to sign specific agreements about not associating with clients socially. But it's professional to maintain some detachment because you're not there to be their friend. You're there to help them be better at their job. The introvert-extrovert dynamic is another reason to be clear about boundaries between trainer and participants. If you're an extrovert, plan time to be with other people to get your energy. If you're an introvert, plan downtime. I'm about 60 percent introvert and 40 percent extrovert. When I'm on the road, I'll work with a group of people, then head straight back to my hotel room. I have a portable speaker and listen to music, sometimes with a glass of wine or a cup of herbal tea depending on how virtuous I feel. If it's a nice enough hotel, I'll sometimes take a hot bath and listen to Mozart. It works wonders and allows me to be my best for the people I'm here to support.

Find Time to Decompress
The human mind and body were not designed to be on the go 24/7. We need downtime, such as sleep to restore bodily functions including muscle growth, tissue repair, protein synthesis, and growth hormones.

And we need to protect ourselves from excessive stress. Studies show that animals deprived of sleep lose all immune function and die within weeks. It's essential that we decompress from the day's busy demands and take time out for restorative action.

I'm amazed how many managers tell me that they are paying staff for annual leave they didn't take. I have to admit, I've never got to the end of the year and found I had use it or lose it vacation time. But many do. I think that managers are wasting their resources by not encouraging staff to take leave. Leave is like an oil change for a car. Their staff are depleting their energy levels when they skip vacations. I understand that sometimes business circumstances conspire against taking leave, but vacations should be a priority.

On a more daily basis, we need to schedule activities that help us decompress. Meditation is a good method; many forms of meditation and relaxation exercises are restorative. If that's not your cup of tea, playing a sport or joining a club can do the trick. Try finding a hobby. In my 40s, I relearned the piano—my piano teachers of yesteryear would be proud—and the piano now acts as my closet therapist, enabling me to detach from work stress and focus on the relaxing rhythm of music. I'm not much chop on the keys, but who cares? It helps me decompress.

At night, I often find myself exhausted but still wired. This makes sleep more difficult. While I'm not advocating for staring at your smartphone screen right before you turn out the lights, I've found that sleep apps help me fall asleep faster. These apps have someone take you through a hypnotic sequence of thoughts that calms you down. I use Pzizz, which has been incredibly helpful for quick naps and battling jetlag. Other relaxation apps you might consider include Meditation for Fidgety Skeptics; Stop, Breathe & and Think; Headspace; and Calm.

You'll find more with a simple Google search. I suggest you also grab some wraparound headphones you can wear while you sleep. Traditional headphones and earbuds can be uncomfortable on a pillow, but wraparounds are like a cushioned towel that wraps around your head and has built-in earphones.

Introduce Physical Activity

I must admit that I'm not much of an exercise person. Pumping iron or running endlessly on a treadmill fills me with no excitement. But trainers can boost their moods (and those of their participants) when they're tired and stressed with some simple exercise. You've seen this in the classroom when you get a tired group of participants to stand up for an activity. Previously slumped and dreary, they're now alert and filled with more energy.

There are all sorts of ways to get high-intensity exercise that helps your brain release endorphins, which will boost your energy. It doesn't have to be running multiple miles or biking to work. I know some people who use the stairs rather than escalators and elevators when they get the chance. We have many options. Despite my aversion to physical activity, I often practice yoga in my hotel because the stretching is fabulous for circulation and helps iron out some of the kinks you get from sitting in airplane seats.

Tai Chi and Qigong are other great options. They are systems of body movements based on set postures that promote deeper breathing and are similar to martial arts exercises. They offer similar benefits to yoga. You'll find routines to follow on YouTube.

Walking is great, too. If you're in a city away from home, a 20-minute walk around the block in the fresh air after class can do wonders to your spirit and get the oxygen and blood flowing. If you're physically exhausted, try sitting on a park bench.

All these tactics assume that you're on the road somewhere or conducting a training class. However, you may be back in the office after a two-week onboarding class doing administrative work. You're tired, grumpy, and dragging your feet. Try taking a laptop to a cafe and working remotely. If that's not possible, swap with a colleague and work at their desk. Can't swap with someone? Book a conference room and set up there for half a day. As they say, a change is as good as a holiday.

Keeping Your Mojo

Back in that training session in North Carolina, I lost my mojo because I'd stretched myself too thin and packed my schedule too tight. As a result, I compromised my professionalism by reacting rather than responding to the participant's question and thus supporting her learning. If I'd better planned my energy and been more realistic when creating my schedule, I could have been truer to my purpose. Unfortunately, life is only getting busier, with emails chasing us 24/7 and clients demanding more of us. Ironically, the only way to do more is to do less, by planning our energy.

10

TRAVEL: TAMING THE UNFRIENDLY SKIES AND INHOSPITABLE HOTELS

I love travel, but hate traffic and planes.
I wish I could just beam myself anywhere instantly.
—Jordan Ladd

YOU'VE PROBABLY HEARD about people falling asleep in class. Heck, you may have had participants catch some *zzzs* or teeter on the edge of nodding off while you're leading a workshop. Now don't worry, I'm not making a judgment call here because it kind of happened to me once. Only it was the other way around. It was midday, and I was facilitating a creativity workshop in Asia. I won't say where in Asia, because I'm still a little embarrassed. But halfway through the day, I nodded off. I was in the corner of the room after lunch. They were doing an exercise and I was visiting slumberland.

My flight from London had arrived at 7:00 the night before, after 13 hours at the back of the plane, traveling economy class. Or as I call it, cattle class, because the way they pack you into economy, I feel like cattle being herded. Shortly after takeoff, they roll through the cabin asking, "Chicken or pasta?" then slap down a tray of something with a cheap half bottle of wine. (Back in the days of US Airways, I got a flight from London Gatwick to Washington Dulles, and I asked the flight attendant if he recommended the chicken or pasta. That was always the option. He said, and I quote, "They don't much taste different.") On this flight to Asia, I was in the back, wedged into a middle seat because I didn't have status on this airline and thus got one of the worse seats. When we landed, my bag was delayed, so I didn't end up leaving the airport until 9 p.m.

None of this is an excuse, though, because I was the one who agreed to facilitate a workshop 14 hours after my plane touched down. So here I was, struggling in the corner to stay awake. Why did I agree to the gig? After all, it's critical that we are our best when we facilitate, which is why, as we discussed in chapter 9, it's critical that we manage our energy. But if you travel a lot, many things conspire against you having the energy to be alert and focused: Your flight. Your hotel. And your planning.

I have to admit that I used to like travel. But now, averaging 150,000 miles of flights a year, much of the charm of jet travel has evaporated. Forget jet lag, red-eye flights, and the other physical things that travel inflicts on our bodies, such as dehydration, fatigue, irritable bowel syndrome, bloating, and the threat of deep vein thrombosis. Flying is just hard work: security checks, waiting at the gate when a flight is delayed, sitting next to someone who doesn't understand personal space or has body odor. Not to mention that you're away from home.

Despite the fact that many hours of learning are delivered virtually, trainers around the globe still find themselves on the road a lot. Travel is hard on our bodies no matter which way you look at it, but we can do a number of things to reduce the discomfort of shuffling on and off airplanes and in and out of hotels several times a week. In the coming pages, I'm going to share what I've learned on the road, plus tips other trainers have shared with me. I focus on air travel rather than going by train or car because that's the experience most of us have.

If someone asked me for my top five travel tips, I'd say:

- Join a loyalty program.
- Pick your flights well.
- Choose your hotels carefully
- Pack wisely.
- Do your admin.

Join a Loyalty Program

One of the best ways to minimize the discomforts of business travel is to join a loyalty program. Airlines, hotel chains, and rental companies all offer them, and the higher your status, the more privileges they offer that make travel much easier.

Loyalty programs generally have several tiers. Hilton's program starts with Member, then moves through Silver and Gold to its top tier, Diamond. Member status is available to anyone who signs up and offers late checkout and discounts on bookings. Late checkout is a neat privilege because very often on multiday programs we're fussing about on the last day to wrap things up. The added tasks of packing and checking out take time and can be stressful. Being able to check out later offers that extra breathing space. When you have stayed 60 nights and satisfied a few other requirements, you earn Diamond status—the top tier—and benefit from things such as space-available room upgrades and 48-hour room guarantees. Perks change from location to location and company to company, but they can help take the edge off travel discomfort.

I'm not an advocate of a particular loyalty program but do advocate choosing one and using it for all your hotel stays and flights. The aim should be to accrue as many miles as you can so you achieve the highest status possible. It does not pay to spread your miles across different loyalty programs. When it comes to flying, the majority of major airlines belong to an alliance of carriers such as Star Alliance, One World, or SkyTeam. You'll earn miles anytime you fly with their partner airlines. I have belonged to United's Mileage Plus for decades. It's a member of the Star Alliance and is convenient for me because I live near Washington Dulles International Airport, a United hub. Folks I know in Atlanta, a hub for Delta, are with SkyMiles. I also signed up for membership with American Airlines' AAdvantage Plus a few years ago but now rarely fly American because it undermines my loyalty strategy. I learned this the hard way.

A few years ago, I accrued 97,000 miles with United—just short of achieving 100K status—and 55,000 with American, enough to get Platinum status. But American Airlines didn't award me Platinum status, because only three of my flights were with American; the rest were with one of their partner airlines, British Airways. I earned the miles, but not the status. I felt ripped off, but when I went and read the fine print, it was there all plain and simple. So, I got no benefits and wished I'd just flown with airlines in the Star Alliance. The lesson here? Read the details in the agreement. Good loyalty programs offer amazing benefits, but you have to know your way around the fine print.

Every airline loyalty program has its unique set of benefits, but most offer one free bag check at the entry levels. As you earn more miles and increase your status, you'll access more perks such as automatic upgrades when a seat is available. You'll also get priority boarding, which is critical for road warriors who choose not to check luggage and need overhead space to stow their carry-on bags. Elite members can access business lounges within their alliance when traveling internationally, regardless of whether you're in business or economy class.

Other benefits come with higher status. United's MileagePlus Program offers members who have flown more than a hundred thousand miles in the previous year, and attain what they call 100k status, a complimentary alcoholic beverage and meal item from the snack cart without charge, when flying in coach. OK, no one is writing home about the meal items in economy, but sometimes it can be very convenient. Most airlines provide priority tags for checked luggage so your bags come out early when you arrive, although my experience is that this is hit and miss. Just last week, in fact, after a flight from Addis Ababa, Ethiopia, to Washington, D.C., the bags with priority tags came out last.

Flying isn't the only way to earn miles. If you sign up for a credit card associated with your loyalty program, you'll earn points every time you spend. While these miles generally don't count toward your tier status, they're great for notching up miles for free flights and upgrades. I use my United credit card for most of my personal purchases and pay it off at the end of the month before they hit me with interest rates. I earn enough miles each year for a business class flight to Australia.

Loyalty has its benefits beyond the airplane ride. Members of United's 100k mileage tier also get free membership in Marriott's Platinum Premier Elite status. On a recent work trip to Dubai, I was staying at a Marriott property where platinum elite members had access to the lounge with free happy hour drinks and appetizers. Some nights, I just didn't want to leave the property to find a restaurant, so the lounge met every need after a long day in the classroom. The lounge also had a boardroom for members to book. I used it for some client and partner meetings, and it made me look professional. It sure beat meeting in a Starbucks.

If there's anything I've learned about life on the road, it's to join a loyalty program and max out its benefits to remove some of those annoying travel hassles. If you're not convinced, think for a moment what travel is like without those perks. You'll be in the last group that boards the airplane unless you have a full first-class ticket. That generally means saying goodbye to overhead space for your carry-on and stuffing it under the seat where you'd prefer to put your feet. Expect to be in a middle seat at the back near the restrooms, where I was on that flight to Asia to teach creativity. If you want to sit up front in economy plus—more legroom, plus you're the first out of the plane—you'll have to pay for the privilege. You'll be charged for checked bags. And when flights are delayed or canceled, airlines help people with status first, so you'll be at the end of the line. Oh, and ever been to the airport when it's busy? A hundred people in line to check their bags? Yeah, that's you. Higher-tier-status members check in with first-class folks, which is almost always quicker.

Pick Your Flights Well

The goal for every trainer is to arrive at their destination fresh and energized, not frazzled and distracted. We owe this to our learners. Some think this is possible simply by leaving and arriving at the right time of the day. However, the difference between a good and bad flight often comes down to the aircraft you're on, its configuration, and whether it is busy.

Many seasoned travelers check to see what aircraft will be flown on their route before buying their ticket; it's listed on the itinerary. The size of the plane is something folks look at because some smaller aircraft, such as Embraer and Canadair Regional Jets, have narrow seats, which are uncomfortable. Some small aircraft require boarding directly from the tarmac up a narrow set of flight stairs, presenting access issues for those who need assistance walking. I like smaller regional aircraft because they're quicker to board and deplane. After a week on the road, all I want to do is get off the aircraft and go home.

Being familiar with the different aircraft that airlines fly can help you choose flights that are easier on your body. I like Boeing's 787 Dreamliner because it's made of carbon-composite materials. Now before you say I'm a plane nerd, there is a reason to know things like this. Airframes in most commercial aircraft are constructed of metal and require operators to have lower humidity levels in the cabin to prevent corrosion. This is what causes nausea and dehydration on long flights. However, carbon composites are not corrosive, so pilots can set humidity levels closer to what we're used to on the ground. This, and a number of other innovations, means we arrive fresher. I thought this was all hype until my first 787 redeye between Bangkok and Delhi. I couldn't believe how good I felt after the flight. I have since flown Dreamliners on multiple 12- to 15-hour routes and always arrive fresh. Many times I hardly feel any jet lag. Being fresh is so important for us to perform well as trainers. I go out of my way to find flights that operate a Dreamliner because I know I'll arrive in better shape.

Another thing to consider when booking is where to sit. Most airlines will allow you to choose your seat. I like aisle seats at the front of the aircraft; they make it easier to access the overhead bin and access the restroom without climbing over someone who wants to sleep. And being at the front means you're out of the plane quicker than when you're seated at the back. Everyone has their preferences; some always want to be by the window. But there's more to seat choice than just aisle and window. How close are you to the restroom? Or galley? It's no fun being close to the galley, where flight attendants talk and make noise preparing meal services, on a redeye flight if you want to sleep. A few years ago, I was in first class in row 1 on a redeye from Washington, D.C., to Geneva. I was feeling all smug because I'd just got an upgrade. However, just feet away was where the attendants had their jump seats, and they spent the entire journey talking about their kids' sports matches. It was horrible, and I couldn't sleep.

And how about the emergency exit? You'll get extra legroom, but often these seats have limited recline. And, does the airline serve meals from front to back or back to front? If you want to be sure not to miss your choice, plan your seat for where the service starts. How can you keep up with all these priorities? Sites like SeatGuru.com reviews seats on just about every airline and are a wealth of information to help you choose the best seat.

As well as seat comfort, look at how busy the flight is when you book, which you can tell by seeing which seats are available. A friend, who mostly flies with Delta, books flights at odd hours because he knows that the first-class cabin will be less booked and his upgrade chance is higher. Others look for flights with a better chance of having a whole row in the economy cabin to themselves.

First, Business, and Economy Class

Tell someone you're flying business class and they'll think you've just entered the life of luxury, but you haven't. First class (on international flights) is about luxury. But business class travel is about avoiding discomfort. While I occasionally get comfortable in economy class, my experience is more often than not one of discomfort. And I find myself playing elbow wars with the person next to me because he encroaches on my personal space. Or I get an up close and personal perspective of their body odor, bad breath, or cheap cologne. On that flight from London to the workshop in Asia, I was wedged between a young guy who smelled like he'd just come from the gym and an older woman who kept falling asleep and slumping across my armrest. Just recently, a friendly man next to me had been eating blue cheese and every time he talked to me, a vaporous aroma of gorgonzola wafted by.

I know I'm not painting a very positive picture of economy class, but it's just not easy to do so. I suppose you could put up with these things if you fly only a few times a year. But many trainers are on and off flights every week. Economy class travel wears thin quickly. It doesn't help that legroom and seat width have shrunk over the past 30 years. Britain's *Daily Telegraph* laid it all out: Thirty years ago, legroom on United was 32 to 36 inches; today, it's 30 to 32 inches (Smith 2018). British Airways long-haul flights had 31 to 34 inches 30 years ago, but today offer 31 inches. It's the same story for seat width. The *Telegraph* said that seats on American were 19 to 20 inches wide 30 years ago. Now, they're 16.5 to 19.3 inches. Southwest was 19 and is now 17. Believe it or not, every inch counts.

Because economy class is just so uncomfortable, I do everything I can to fly first class domestic in the United States or business class on international flights. I'm not fussed for flights of just a few hours and happily travel economy. But flights longer than two or three hours, where you are seated with your elbows pinned to your side with a passenger in front reclining their seat onto your knees, take a physical toll. The value of first-class travel in the United States is not the service or food they sometimes provide, which is generally hit or miss. It's the extra seat width and legroom that allows you to arrive with fewer aches and pains. And the space it offers to work on your laptop—how many times have you found yourself needing to change or even start your PowerPoint deck on your flight to the location where you'll deliver training? Sitting in smaller seats for prolonged periods is not good for your back, and while this may be a symptom of me just getting old, the seats are getting more and more uncomfortable. How would the company's health and safety office react if you sat at your desk for three hours straight, bunched up, not allowed to move? Carpal tunnel, crook back, and all sorts of other ailments would be ringing alarm bells for the workers' compensation insurance. Yet it's apparently OK at 36,000 feet.

The easiest way to get a first-class ticket is to ask your boss or client to pay for it. I know, your boss might say no, because she thinks you just want to live a jet-set lifestyle. It may be worth a conversation about how the accumulation of bad flights could cost the company in terms of worse feedback from training programs and more sick days as you recover from aches, pains, and illnesses. If that fails, devote your effort to boosting your status in your airline loyalty program so you get automatic upgrades or enough miles to put toward flying up front. When you check in, carriers often offer deals to get into the first-class cabin; $150 is worth it to fly first class from Denver to New York if it avoids a chiropractic visit. These days, I don't fly more than five hours for work unless it's business class.

International business class is equivalent to domestic first class, only better. (International first class is a cut up from that, although I don't personally think it's worth the extra money. But it does get you a bigger seat, better wines, and sometimes better food.) If you're flying a long distance, the important thing is to have a seat that stretches into a lie-flat bed so you can sleep. The business-class cabins on most airlines these days offer lie-flat seats, so I think first class is hard to justify.

Business class tickets are not always cheap. But the money you save on these flights will cost you elsewhere, like your health and less powerful learning for your attendees. Longer flights in business class mean you arrive refreshed, focused, and alert. This makes you a better trainer.

Airports

The increased security at airports since 9/11 has made travel cumbersome, so much so that you can be exhausted before you even board the aircraft. There are ways to make it easier.

Choose the time you fly. I try to fly in the middle of the day. In my experience, most people shoot for early morning or early evening commuter flights, so airports are manic before 9 a.m. and after 3 p.m. It's much less frantic from 10 a.m. to 2 p.m., and security lines takes less time to go through. I always try to fly the day before a workshop because it takes some pressure off. If you fly in the middle of the day and your flight is canceled or delayed, there's a good chance you'll find a later flight. Fly later in the day and you risk being stranded.

Also, try to fly through or to smaller airports when you can. Larger airports like Dulles, O'Hare, or JFK require lots of walking and sometimes catching trains between terminals. Smaller airports are quick and easy to navigate, and in my experience the staff are friendlier and less hassled. In Washington, D.C., Reagan National Airport is almost a joy to fly into compared with Dulles. It doesn't take too long to get to the gate or find a restaurant, and security lines are generally fast. If you're flying home to a small airport such as National, you'll be at the cab station five minutes after you leave the plane.

Choose airports that offer conveniences that you need. My favorite airport, Singapore Airport, offers excellent food, shopping, showers, therapeutic massages, and a mini hotel in the terminal to get three or four hours' rest on a real bed between flights. If I'm connecting through Asia, I always try to do so through this airport and have a set routine. I get a deep-tissue massage to soothe aching muscles after having slept in a bad posture. Then I go to the mini hotel and book a room for four hours for a quick shower and a few hours of real sleep in a real bed. It's amazing how much better that makes you feel.

You can learn about what airports offer and don't through quick online searches, then choose flights based on where you connect. With the exception of the Senator Lounge and bookshop opposite, I loathe Frankfurt Airport. It's big, has a confusing layout and I have lost count of the times staff in the security line have been rude to me. I do whatever I can to find flights that don't connect through Frankfurt. But I truly love the Munich Airport. It's clean, efficient, and so quiet you can hear a pin drop, so I'll jump on any flight connecting through Munich. When choosing a flight that connects through other airports, check for lounges and other facilities, such as showers. Read reviews beforehand because some lounges at some airports are not great. Mid-tier status with most airline loyalty programs will get you access to airport lounges while connecting on international flights.

Sign up for fast-track programs. In the United States you can beat the long security lines by getting TSA pre-check. They don't ask you to take your shoes off unless they have metal in them, and you can keep laptops in your briefcase. I know these things don't seem like much, but when you're on the road they mean a lot. If you travel internationally, sign up for Global Entry and you'll be able to skip the immigration line, instead using a computerized kiosk that scans your passport. When you apply, the TSA will perform a background check on you and if you pass, allow you to use the Global Entry lines at participating airports. I love it; immigration never takes more than five or 10 minutes.

Not everyone wants to spend the extra money on Global Entry, especially if most of their travel is domestic. If that's you, but you want immigration to be fast on those few trips you take overseas, learn to speed walk. I'm serious. After a long flight, most passengers are still hazy-headed. You'll see this in the way they walk off the plane. This is the time to suck in your breath and charge forward, walking as fast as you can past them all. They won't even notice you, and you're effectively jumping up the line. Until I had Global Entry, speed walking was my strategy to get through immigration and customs fast. And it always worked.

Choose Your Hotels Carefully

Did you know that when you stay in a hotel bed, your body sheds 1.5 million cells or cell clusters an hour? If you get six hours' sleep, that's 9 million in a night. I'm only talking about what you leave behind because it's a nicer thought than what's been left for you by the folks who stayed in your room the night before. Or the past month. We talked about hotels in the last chapter, so we won't spend much time here other than two areas to keep your energy up and avoid getting ill.

According to CNN, hotel rooms are full of human hair, bodily secretions, fungi, bacteria, dust, insect parts, pollen, cosmetics, and more (Hunter 2011). Do a Google search and you'll find that bedspreads are the worst carriers of nasty stuff because in some of the less premium hotel chains, they're hardly ever washed.

Travel exposes us to all sorts of germs and bacteria, so to be on our game, we need to ramp up our defenses. I know folks who carry Clorox bleach wipes with them to wipe down common surfaces previous guests are likely to have touched. You have no idea whether past guests have cleaned their hands or covered their mouths when coughing in the room. I don't carry bleach wipes with me, because most hotels I choose are OK. But there are some hotels where I've done an about turn, upon seeing the lack of cleanliness, and headed to Walgreens for heavy-duty cleaning materials. Start with the phone—yes, we still use hotel phones for room service or to call the front desk, and a lot of people spit into the mouthpiece when they talk without knowing it. Clean the door handles, faucets, and flush handle on the toilet. Clean the remote control for the television; there are all sorts of little cracks where happy bacteria love to live.

Being conscious of hygiene is one way to stay healthy. Another thing to keep in mind is diet. When you eat in restaurants all the time or scarf down free breakfasts in hotel lobbies, you have little control over how much sugar and other additives find their way into your meal. I like hotels with kitchenettes, like Residence Inns. I follow the ketogenic diet, so cooking my own meals and breakfast allows me to eat the way I know will keep me healthy and energized. I look for hotels close to a supermarket for convenience, although some chains, like the Residence Inn, take grocery lists and shop for you while you are at the office.

Pack Wisely

Travel is much easier when you don't need to check a bag at the airport. There's no chance your luggage will be lost, so you minimize the chance of finding yourself at the front of a class in jeans and a sweatshirt. Even when it's not lost, it can sometimes take a long time to find its way to the baggage belt, like when I did that workshop in Asia. Another reason for carrying on is you'll have everything you need to stay fresh if you miss a connection and have to grab a hotel before your final destination. And you can leave the airport almost immediately after you land. If there's one decision that made my travel life easier, it was packing everything into a carry-on.

To avoid checking a bag, you need to squeeze everything into your carry-on and personal bag. The carry-on is generally your roll-on, and the personal item is your briefcase or purse. Here are a few things I consider when packing for the road, with a training focus:

- Pack two pairs of shoes: one for the classroom, and a comfy set for the evening to help reset after standing on your feet all day. Wear the biggest shoes when flying to save space in your carry-on.

- Pack clothes with colors that mix and match. Some folks like to pack all black because it's easy to match. But other neutral colors are a great idea.
- Travel with iron-free pants, skirts, shirts, and blouses. Hang them in the shower and let the steam take wrinkles away.
- Pack comfy clothes for long-haul flights. I wear track pants with an elastic waist on long flights and a comfy sweater.
- Pack travel-sized toiletries like toothpaste, deodorant, and shaving cream from the drugstore. Consider using hotel shampoo and soap, if you can stand them.
- Pack some medical supplies. I carry Advil, bandages, heartburn pills, and other things in case I'm not feeling well.
- If you pack a suit, wear the jacket onboard rather than squish it in your carry-on. In first class, flight attendants will hang it for you. Some flight attendants in coach will, too, if you ask nicely.
- Remember chargers for your laptop, phone, and tablet. You can save space by taking only one charger and using it for your tablet and phone in turn.
- Pack back-up classroom tools, such as a remote-control clicker for PowerPoint slides, whiteboard markers, and flipchart pens.

Do Your Admin

To travel comfortably, you need to plan well. Much of that can be done with apps and cloud software. And while the apps can make it easier, knowing which ones to use can be a dilemma.

Make sure you have the app for your preferred carrier. For example, United's app tells me which gate I'm flying to and from, which luggage belt to fetch my bags from, the seat map so I can see if I'm on my own, the upgrade list, the flight status, and even where my aircraft comes from. You can also use it to check in, change seats, or find another flight.

Hotels offer apps as well. Hilton's app allows you to check in, choose the room you want, and even unlock the door to your room. It has options to order extra pillows, your favorite snack, or a beverage. These are just a few things that make travel easier, and if you're a member of loyalty programs, you can enter your preferences. Some hotels ask if you'd like soft or hard pillows.

It's helpful to collect all your itinerary details in one place. TripIt is a helpful online app that collates your travel plans. Email the booking confirmations to TripIt, and it will create an automated itinerary. The paid version will alert you when flights are delayed and give your significant other access to the account so they can see travel details. You can print a paper version of your itinerary before leaving home, in case your battery dies.

Being Strategic With Your Travel

How would it have been if, on that trip to run a creativity workshop somewhere in Asia, I'd flown on an airline that was part of my loyalty program? If I'd gotten an aisle seat, rather than a middle seat? Been closer to the front? Packed everything into my carry-on so I didn't have to wait two hours for my bag when I arrived at the airport? Allowed a day in the country to beat the jet lag? Or have insisted on a business class-ticket? Most likely, I wouldn't have nodded off.

Like a lot of things in training, we make a bigger thing of our failures than others do. I apologized to the organizer, who was surprised. "You nodded off?" she asked. "I didn't see you." Apparently the group was so busy with their exercise, my momentary lapse was not noticed. Lucky, I'd had them working hard to build their learning, otherwise they would have seen me.

Travel is not easy. And it gets harder the more we find ourselves on the road. Working across time zones and dealing with the physiological impact of being in an aircraft and a hotel takes its toll. That's why it pays to be smart about every part of your journey. You may not make it fun, but you'll minimize the damage.

APPS FOR THE ROAD WARRIOR

Many apps are designed to support frequent travelers. They're being constantly updated and new ones are launched all the time. So use Google to stay abreast. Here are some great apps to consider now:

- **Rideshare services:** Essential for booking rides around town, just about everyone has Uber or Lyft these days. What's cool is they email you your receipt.
- **PackPoint:** Based on your destination and the weather, it will help you build a packing list before you go.
- **XE Currency Converter:** Don't blindly spend money in another currency. XE will give you the latest currency conversions.
- **Google Translate:** This app helps you communicate conversationally in more than 100 languages.
- **Expensify:** Capture expense receipts on the run, rather than stuffing them into your pocket and briefcase to add up when you get home. It will even submit expenses to the appropriate person.
- **MyTSA:** This shows which airports and terminals have TSA checkpoint lines.
- **HotelTonight:** They promise to book a hotel in under 10 seconds. If you miss your connection and the airline doesn't give you a hotel, this app will help.
- **GateGuru:** Access information about restaurants, shops, and amenities in most airports around the world. Land in Chicago and need a Chicago Dog? In Heathrow and want to find Harrods? Check GateGuru.
- **AwardWallet:** This app keeps track of mileage points across all your programs and will remind you when they are about to expire, so you don't lose them.

A Trainer Recounts a Travel Horror Story

Halelly Azulay

WHEN THE ANNOUNCEMENT SPEAKER at the major Virginia airport warned that bad weather in Dallas was creating flight delays and cancellations, my anxiety level began to rise. After all, I was in the terminal awaiting my flight to an extremely high-stakes training program.

That's how my client had described this particular group and the program they were sending me to onboard in Dallas. It's a pilot program, they explained. Lots of VIPs will be scrutinizing it, and its results could really make-or-break their ability to continue this initiative. If it's successful, that'll mean more training programs for the next iterations to follow. Don't screw it up, they stressed, a lot is riding on it.

It was Sunday, and my mid-day flight should have left me plenty of time to get into my Dallas hotel, have dinner, and prepare for the early start on Monday. Except, the weather had other plans. Powerless, I watched flight after flight get canceled.

Incredibly, I was finally able to get onto the stand-by list for the last flight scheduled for Dallas that day (and the first flight to actually leave). I ended up being the fourth and last stand-by passenger to be allowed on board. The catch? They couldn't let me carry my rollaboard suitcase onto the plane—it was completely full. Oh well.

Once we pulled out of the gate and began taxiing (phew!), the pilot announced that our plane was overweight and that we'd be returning to the gate to offload some bags "randomly." Fast forward to landing. You might already have guessed this, but I was told that my bag—being the last to be loaded on—was one of those randomly pulled off. It would only arrive tomorrow, the gate attendant said.

Gulp. I stood there wearing jeans, a simple T-shirt, and scuffed-up clogs. My bag had all my toiletries, my makeup, and my outfit for the high-stakes training tomorrow morning. It was past 10 on a Sunday night, and no stores were open for me to buy a new outfit. I couldn't even shop in the morning either because I had to be on the client site at 7 a.m.

The day of I powered through and kicked off the program in my jeans and T-shirt "look," using some self-deprecating humor. I told a bit of my travel story to show vulnerability and try to soften the shock of my unprofessional appearance.

How did it go? I'm really happy to report that I was able to pull it off despite this obstacle and delivered an engaging, spotless performance. The client was happy, the program was a smashing success, and we've been getting return business for it for more than five years now. Yay for happy endings.

My biggest lesson learned: Always wear something on business travel that I would be comfortable having to work in the next morning. And have spare makeup in my briefcase!

Halelly Azulay is author of Employee Development on a Shoestring *and* Strength to Strength: How Working From Your Strengths Can Help You Lead a More Fulfilling Life. *She also hosts the popular Talent Grow podcast.*

11

REMAINING CLEAR-HEADED WHEN THE NEXT TREND STRIKES

*Great things are not accomplished by those who yield
to trends and fads and popular opinion.*
—Jack Kerouac

I DON'T USUALLY like to tell many people, but I was once completely caught up in the organic food wave. Every Tuesday, a heavy brown box filled with organic vegetables was left on the doorstep of our house on Fitzjohn Avenue, in London. We never knew what vegetables they'd deliver but the mystery was half the fun. We paid 25 quid a week, and they always packed it with vegetables that were in season and locally grown. We felt good about it and held our heads high, knowing that by spending a little extra money, we were saving ourselves from ingesting nasty chemicals with our broccoli. Or were we?

I discovered the real story when a friend accused me of being a bourgeois fool. We were at a party in someone's London flat, and he laughed when I told him my wife and I ate organic. "Organic food is a scam!" he said, chewing on a pretzel. "It's no healthier than regular produce." My friend wasn't a conspiracy nut, so I took what he said seriously. When I got home later that night, I did some online research, and well, I was shocked. Many newspapers, including reputable publications such as the UK's *Independent* newspaper, the *Washington Post,* and *Scientific American,* had published articles debunking the notion that organic food was healthier than regular produce. Some even called it a myth. As I dug deeper, I found that organic farms actually do use pesticides. How could that be possible? An article on the *Scientific American* website explained they get away with using them based on "the origin of the pesticides used" (Wilcox 2011). Another assumption shattered. And I was stunned at how many studies suggested that there were little to no health benefits from eating organic over regular produce. It was hard to believe; the notion that organic food was healthier simply made so much sense to me. I couldn't believe I'd fallen for this trend. Worse still, I had been paying a premium for food that wasn't making me any healthier than regular produce.

It's easy to make decisions based on what appears to be common sense. Millions are swept up in the latest diet, exercise routine, or investment strategy. Some of them actually are effective, while others merely make us believe they'll work because they seem true on the surface but lack a solid foundation. Of course, trend waves sweep through the training world, too. Some are long waves that last a decade or longer; others last six months. But they influence the decisions people make and the money they spend all the same. Take learning styles, an instructional approach that has been around for many years. It was one of those longer waves that heavily influenced adult education and school teaching. I've lost count of how many people still believe it when I lead train-the-trainer workshops. Learning styles and all the attending assumptions roll easily off the tongue and sound credible, much like organic food being healthier sounds credible. On the surface, it makes sense: Some people learn visually, some auditorily, and some kinesthetically. Right? It seems so obvious. But dig into the research, like I did with organic food, and it's tough to find rigorous evidence to support it. And learning styles isn't the only theory in our profession that has been revered or become popular without evidence. Take left-right brain theory. Generational differences. Neuro-this and neuro-that.

Learning theories aren't the only things that sweep through. Buzzwords are another; our profession is full of them. Take, for example, what we call ourselves. Over the years, we've had titles etched on business cards that describe us as facilitators, workplace learning professional—a mouthful, I admit, but descriptive—instructors, guides, sherpas, and more. One year it's this; the next it's that. I know there are reasons for the different words we use for the work of the "common trainer," but my point is that buzzwords come and go. The current big buzzword is *microlearning*. There's not really any strong consensus among experts about what microlearning is. But go to any learning conference and you'll hear people throwing the term around as if they're practicing for the school play.

Another thing we see come in waves are the frameworks that training companies license trainers to administer in their practices. You hear comments at conferences like, "I administer the 4-Step Inno-Leadership Framework for executives." It sounds very impressive and official. I've lost count of how many different frameworks come and go in popularity, often based on bestselling business books. One year everyone wants to do the 4-Step Framework, then next year a new framework pushes that out and people get busy being licensed in that one. Put the prefix *neuro* in front of it, and the wave might last a little longer. (By the way, before you go Google the 4-Step Inno-Leadership Framework, I have to confess: I made it up. I just didn't want to use a real methodology in case the company that owns it sues me for being cynical.) Now here's a caveat: Just because these things come in waves doesn't mean they're ineffective. Quite the contrary; many are terrific and provide people and organizations with tremendous value. But many others don't.

INSIDER TIP

Looking for a concise critique on the key learning theories bandied around the profession? Clark Quinn's book *Millennials, Goldfish & Other Training Misconceptions* is a great start. In fact, I think it belongs on every trainer's bookshelf because it reviews key learning theories based on evidence.

Why Are These Waves So Prevalent?

The yearly wave of theories, buzzwords, and frameworks confuses and distracts people no matter their industry or discipline. So why do they keep rolling in? A cynical response might be that shiny new ideas lead to fame and fortune. For example, a new buzzword comes along. No one has written a book about it, and because it's so new, there's hardly any research on it to dispute it. Write that book, give it a catchy title, and you instantly become the industry expert. Airport bookstores are full of these types of books, and you'll be on the speaking circuit at $40k a speech in no time.

A less cynical reason is the way these frameworks tie complex ideas into tidy bundles that are easy to conceptualize and make sense of because they share a language that gives confidence. Of course, complex ideas are more often than not nonlinear and don't always lend themselves to tidy definitions, acronyms, or abbreviations. But our brains crave orderly definition, so if these frameworks make sense on the surface, they are attractive. In addition to the models being effective, the language associated with them adds an air of credibility and makes us more self-assured.

But there's another reason why these waves sweep us off our feet: I can't help but wonder if it's because we don't conduct our due diligence. Instead, we adopt a method, theory, or technique after reading about it on a blog or in a three-page magazine article but don't have time to check that it's robust. One complaint I always hear from trainers in workshops or at conferences is their lack of time. So, this makes some sense. Or perhaps, and I'm about to be provocative here, we don't have the training to critically evaluate the idea in terms of how it will support learning and performance. Think about it: Many new trainers are thrown into their roles as a reaction to circumstances. I don't know anyone I have worked with who said they wanted to be a trainer when they grew up. They usually say they fell into training—a role they nevertheless love but was still something they hadn't planned.

A typical journey to becoming a trainer goes like this. The boss sees a member of staff explaining to a colleague how to use a piece of equipment or perform a task. The boss thinks, "Gee, she's good at communicating," and suggests she become a trainer. She has a degree in engineering or a trade certification but no background in the science of learning. In the workplace, that doesn't seem to be a problem. Compare this with elementary or high school where you generally need a teaching license, which can take a year to earn on top of an undergraduate degree. But to be a trainer? Our companies send us off on three-day train-the-trainer workshops, which are only really long enough to teach us some basic presentations skills and practice using a flipchart. Within weeks of attending the training workshop, after learning the current buzzwords and superficial things like what point size to use for

PowerPoint text, the trainer is dropped in at the deep end, delivering a four-week onboarding class. Shockingly, some trainers don't even get the train-the-trainer program right away—I've had participants in my advanced workshops tell me they've been training folks for 10 years but never completed formal training in training. They have read lots of books. But they never had the chance to build knowledge and learn the skills of learning.

To properly evaluate each new idea, a fundamental understanding of learning and how it takes place is required. And it should be gained preferably before being thrown to the wolves in a four-week onboarding class. This fundamental understanding is just as important as the average train-the-trainer program, if not more, and something you can't learn by simply asking yourself, *Who was my favorite trainer or teacher?* and then copying their style. No, it comes from lots of deep reading, practice, and reflection. Without a critical understanding of learning and some core theories that have been tested by evidence, it's impossible not to be sucked into a new wave every year.

INSIDER TIP

Where should you go for a list of techniques that aren't fads but really support learning? Ruth Colvin Clark's *Evidence-Based Training Methods* debunks some common myths about learning that have dogged our profession and outlines what we should do to ensure workplace learning.

It concerns me that our profession puts a lot of new trainers in difficult positions because we don't give them the proper foundation. We think, *She's confident in front of a group* or *He's a good communicator,* so we assume they'll make a good trainer and then send them to a three-day class. But think about this for a moment: Would you let someone give you financial advice after a three-day workshop in finance and legal matters? Diagnose medical symptoms at the doctor's office with just a few days' training? Yet we expect trainers to advise managers and their teams about learning and performance issues, which connect directly to an organization's ability to provide goods and services.

Our profession doesn't encourage enough personal professional development. Ironically, we tell clients and leaders of our organizations that they need to put time aside for training, but how many hours of learning do we invest in for ourselves? How many learning executives tell their staff to undertake two weeks' training every year? I ask trainers this question at conferences and in my workshops and hear time and time again that it just doesn't happen. My workshops are often the first professional development opportunity they've had in years. It's like the cobbler's children. The old fable goes that the only children in town without shoes were the cobbler's children. The cobbler was busy making shoes for everyone else and neglected his kids.

Training attracts incredibly talented, resourceful, and creative people. And these people do amazing work. But so many do so without the support they need to really let their creative resourcefulness take off. And without the foundations to be really discerning about these waves that crash into our work every year.

The Science of Learning Is Where It's At

All this takes us back to the central dilemma for trainers and workplace learning professionals who watch this wave of new ideas roll in every year: Which ones are worth adopting or following? I think we can discern this only by being clear about what will change and what won't. And something that will not change, regardless of whether you employ learning styles, accelerated learning, emotional intelligence, or another technique, is the mechanics of learning. This has not changed in millennia—just as a blacksmith or wool weaver in the Industrial

Revolution had to learn their skills through deliberate practice, carefully perfecting their craft over time, people today still need to process memories and new input to build learning. Until technology allows us to copy and paste knowledge and skills from a USB stick directly into the brain, this will be the case. We need to evaluate new ideas based on how they engage the process of cognition. That needs to be the foundation to avoid being swept away. What we're really getting at is the science of learning.

The term *science of learning* is bandied around a lot these days, and I suspect it's one of the waves that will continue to sweep our profession. I think this is a good thing because our profession has in the past been held captive by myths and superstitions about learning that have not helped us deliver what we promise. And science provides a rigorous methodology to steer our practice toward methods that are proven to get results and can give us greater confidence with our clients.

What a lot of people refer to as the science of learning draws heavily on cognitive psychology and neuroscience. You've probably picked up in the subtext of this book that cognitive psychology informs a lot of my practice as a trainer. I've been teaching cognitive learning strategies as a practitioner to corporate trainers since 2000, and I get excited because every year new research strengthens many of its core principles. During the past 20 years, the discipline of neuroscience has grown, fueled by more effective brain-scanning technology, giving us even more insight into how the brain works and what that means for learning.

I believe that every trainer should be grounded in the science of learning. It will give them precision in practice and discernment in knowing what is hype and what is real. And I hope this is the new wave that helps us avoid being swept away by other waves that sound or look good but offer nothing new.

But Let's Not Be Religious About Science

The danger of any wave, whether it is microlearning or right brain–left brain theory, is that it's easy to develop an almost reverent regard for it because it simply seems like common sense. If learning science is the next wave, as I think it might be, it too risks metamorphosing into an almost religious dogma where everything we do must be subject to the canons of science. Learning methods without the science label applied will be disregarded. But it's important to remember that even science is not infallible. Sometimes it's dodgy, other times influenced by professional culture, and still other times, just lacking.

There are many instances where so-called science has been blindly adopted into life, much as we adopted learning styles into the classroom. Take, for example, a study conducted by the University of Virginia in 2015. A key principle of the scientific method of inquiry is that research needs to be reproducible. In that spirit, researchers set out to reproduce the findings of 98 psychology papers. They were only able to reproduce 39 of them, casting serious doubt on more than half of the papers (Baker 2015). Which of those papers, now in doubt, have been used as the basis for other research studies?

Prevailing culture has also been known to prevent good science. Research should be based on objective observation, free from the influence of one's personal leanings or cultural interests. This is certainly what two Australian scientists believed when they discovered that peptic ulcers could be treated with antibiotics. But the mainstream thinking at the time was that stress and diet caused ulcers; it took decades to convince the scientific community, using well-documented data and evidence that this new treatment was more effective.

Some ideas are good but haven't been researched, so we ignore them. Take acupuncture. As a medical treatment it was until recently looked at with disdain by contemporary evidence-based medical experts. But Chinese doctors have been successfully treating patients with it for 2,500 years. Only in the late 1990s did the National Institutes of Health announce that it was good preventative care for nausea and vomiting, suggesting issues such as stroke rehabilitation, addictions, headaches, menstrual cramps, tennis elbow, and muscle pain could be addressed as well. No evidence for something that works? Western medicine was more than 2,000 years late.

INSIDER TIP

You often hear people saying something is backed by science. But what is science? And does science really prove something is right or wrong? In his classic tome *What's This Thing Called Science?*, Alan F. Chalmers explains the scientific method, its strengths and weaknesses, and some of the recent influences on what we think science is.

If you're looking for me to say that science and learning are clear-cut, you may be disappointed. I just said that we need to rigorously check any new trend against the science of learning, but then pointed out how science has failed some situations. There really is no precise way to approach this. We simply need to be discerning and evaluate new ideas based on learning science. Learning science, in my mind, is important for our industry to learn and be proficient at but we also need to resist the temptation to accept anything under the learning science banner without critically reviewing it. We need to ask questions like, what methodology was used for this study? How were the results tabulated? How big were the samples; were they reliable? What did other studies show? Are there other studies, or is this it? And every once in a while, we'll need to make a gut decision about a new idea because no one has gotten around to conducting research on that idea just yet, but it seems sensible and gets results.

Is It Only Science?

A lot of people have fond memories of a great teacher who helped them learn or transformed their lives in some way. They describe them in almost spiritual terms: "She was inspiring" or "He understood my true potential." None of these descriptions are terribly scientific, and you won't find them listed in job descriptions—how do you quantify inspiring? In fact, I haven't even looked into what scientific research might exist on the elements of inspiring teachers. But these teachers are the opposite of the three piano teachers I talked about in chapter 2, who fired me. Remember, one even told me she was a dragon.

Back in chapter 2, I didn't tell you how the story finished. After the third piano teacher fired me, my mother found a new teacher, and she remained my piano teacher until I left high school. She never fired me. She helped me discover how amazing the piano is as an instrument. I attended lessons every Friday night with my brother, and she inspired me to practice and my brother to go on to become a professional jazz pianist. She got us doing deliberate practice—that's how to learn. But she used other personal qualities to motivate and encourage us. That's what I call the art of teaching.

The premise of Elaine Biech's bestselling book on learning, *The Art and Science of Training* (2017), suggests we need to find a balance in our practice between art and science. In my mind, I see the art as being how you deliver the learning and the science as what you do to ensure the learning. Put another way, the science explains what kind of glue I need to join two pieces of wood and why. The art is how I join them to make a beautiful piece of furniture. I haven't spent too much time in this book talking about the art of training because I think many in our profession get the art side pretty well. It's the science side we need to strengthen.

Dislodging the Fads

So where does that leave us?

At this point I should probably confess where I'm at when it comes to organic food. My faith in the whole organic food enterprise was certainly shattered when my friend called me a bourgeois fool, followed by those alarming articles showing that pesticides are used in organic farming. But I'm not totally off the wagon. You'll find organic, cage-free eggs and chicken in our fridge. When possible, it's also stocked with grass-fed beef, and certainly the grass-fed Irish butter they sell in supermarkets, to—it simply tastes too good. But I'm no longer captive to the organic wave and approach my groceries with much more free-dom and skepticism. I don't get as worried when I'm served chicken at a restaurant that doesn't say cage-free. I like to think that's also how I approach new theories, buzzwords, and frameworks.

As learning professionals, it's easy to be swept along by the waves in our profession, but if we maintain a level of critical awareness, based on a foundational knowledge of what learning is and how it happens, we can be sure that we won't get caught up in the latest fad and instead offer real value to the people and organizations we serve. It comes down to knowing the science of learning and then artfully putting it into practice.

12

A TRAINER'S CRYSTAL BALL

It's not in the stars to hold our destiny, but in ourselves.
—William Shakespeare

BEING A FUTURIST has to be the coolest of jobs. You get to read all day, monitor social and technological developments, and then dream about tomorrow. People look to your sage wisdom as you sit on panels at conferences, share your thoughts, nod wisely, and then get hailed as a thought leader. Then, years later, when those predictions were supposed to arrive, everyone has forgotten what exactly you claimed might happen; whether you were on the money or not fades to an afterthought. At any rate, you either are making new predictions, or have parlayed that fame into an early retirement, watching sunsets on a beach in the Caribbean.

This book is not about the future; it's an inside look at a trainer's life. An unashamedly personal take from several decades of work spanning more than 25 countries. I've poked fun at how we do things, questioned some of the practices we see as gospel truths, and explored some core values around workplace learning that have informed my practice. Everything is based on my experience, which is by definition in the past. In this chapter, I'll proffer some humble, but no doubt opinionated, thoughts on what I think our profession might look like in a few years' time.

First, I need to exercise caution because I'm no futurist. And even if I were, futurists don't always anticipate the curve balls history throws at us. After all, who predicted technological innovations like YouTube? Facebook? The smartphone? Not only have futurists failed to predict key things that have revolutionized our lives, they've gotten a lot wrong when they did try. In 1920, the *New York Times* pontificated, "A rocket will never go to the moon." So much for that prediction. In 1912, Marconi, who invented the radio said, "The coming of the wireless era will make war impossible, because it will make war ridiculous. In 1997, a *Wired Magazine* editorial boldly stated to Apple, "Admit it, you're out of the hardware game." Apple is the biggest company in the world. And remember those predictions at the end of the 1990s that face-to-face training would be dead within 10 years and replaced by e-learning? Yeah, 18 years later that still hasn't happened.

To be fair, it's easy to get predictions wrong. That's why when people get them right, they're hailed as world-class thinkers and led around the conference keynote circuit. But it's better to take a stab at the future than fail to anticipate change. So, for what it's worth, here are my thoughts about what's around the corner. They're not exhaustive but rather a snapshot of what's going on in my head, based on the wisdom that many in our profession have shared at conferences, in blog posts, and in conversations. Come find me in 10 years if any of these predictions come true. With any luck, you'll find me watching the sunset with my wife on a beach in the Caribbean.

Where We've Come From

When I started in the training world, back in the early 1990s, training was predominantly conducted in the classroom. PowerPoint slides had just started to replace acetates on overhead projectors, course materials were published in thick, heavy binders, and instructors tended to be more qualified and experienced in their subject than the art and science of instruction. Most would attend train-the-trainer classes, and the lucky few (of which I was one) were able to earn undergraduate teaching degrees in adult learning. Many trainers designed their own classes. If a request was made for a class on a subject, the trainer would grab the leading book on that topic and turn it into a class. Or they'd buy an off-the-shelf program that was probably based on that book and deliver it.

Our organizations were not always endeared to the training department. Some people thought trainers were the folks who couldn't do. Or, burned out on the job, they'd be sent to sit out their retirement in training. The training department was often that quiet office at the end of the corridor, through smoky-yellow glass that had a notice sticky-taped to the glass saying "Out at lunch." I remember interviewing a candidate for a training manager position who told me he got into training because he wanted a quieter life and no shift work. (He didn't get the job.) While this more models the mindset of trainers going back 40 or 50 years, many trainers have leaned into this caricature, despite the existence of phenomenal trainers and training departments.

As a result, many training departments today face existential questions about what they do, how they do it, and what value they provide. They exist in organizations that don't understand how training can help staff work better, where leaders believe our expertise extends only as far as offering boilerplate products like workshops and online learning, rather than tailored solutions that can help the business grow. Fortunately, this has changed in many organizations, but not all.

I think we're in the middle of a seismic shift in workplace learning that started about 15 to 20 years ago, when executives started asking training leaders to show their value. I think we all understand this and are expecting more to come, which it will. However, a storm of external dynamics will influence many of these changes in ways that will surprise us. These dynamics include technology, societal values and norms, regulatory environments, and politics. To get a sense of where we're at, let's think about the organization.

The Future of Training: What Organizations Want

Fueled by the ubiquitous nature of data and analytics, organizations over the past 15 to 20 years have started to demand more from the money they spend on training and talent. As such, many progressive learning departments are rising to the challenge and looking at learning differently: They're thinking innovatively about how to deliver what their organizations want. In many cases, the needs are complex and driven by the need for the organization to be agile in a changing global economy. Here's what we can see already:

Training is no longer about the event. It's about the business results that arise from the event of learning. In the past, trainers, located under HR, offered stakeholders a set catalog of programs to choose from, starting conversations with "I've got a program that covers X that I can offer you." Now trainers, as a true business support function, will ask stakeholders, "What problems are making it hard to meet your business goals?" They'll then design tailored solutions.

This is our future: spending more time with managers and learners to understand what they really need and then developing dynamic ways to help them meet those goals beyond the classroom experience. It's about how trainers improve performance in the workplace. As such, trainers will become experts in performance and the science of skill development, articulating the journey from novice to expert. While the classroom may be one situational tool a trainer uses to help the learner on their journey, they will switch between consulting, teaching, coaching, and creating and curating content. Training solutions, enabled by technology, will be offered at a time that best suits the learner, when they need it, and where it suits them to do the learning. This includes more just-in-time learning with microlearning content. (I could go beyond general trends and mention products and specific apps, but they'll be out of date before the books goes to print.) Learning events will be scheduled closer to deployment, such as new technology roll-outs, so learners can more immediately engage in deliberate practice. Long-term planning of programs won't go away entirely because succession planning will still be important in many companies, but trainers will be responding more and more to immediate business needs. We hear a lot about these things in articles and at conferences as people talk about social learning and the learning ecosystem.

Content is no longer about workbooks and PowerPoint slides. More and more in the future it will be about video, audio, and written content for web posts available anywhere, anytime, on any device, and on the learner's terms. But not just any video—learning professionals will need to learn the grammar of making media as much as the art of facilitating in a classroom. Soon, media will be a mix of more specialized forms of video, augmented and virtual reality, and integration with the Internet of Things. Before long, learning content will be embedded in everyday things beyond the formal model we have today.

The big picture is that we're shifting from a world where we deliver training products to one in which we help people in the business work better. I know some may argue that delivering training products helps people work better, but the subtle difference in nuance emphasizes that it's not about us or our product, but about the learner and how they do their job.

Many talent development and training departments are smaller than they were 15 years ago. To make up for this, social learning and microcontent with digital media such as video and podcasts will continue to grow and be championed not just by learning evangelists but leaders throughout the organization. Because of this, employees will have a bigger stake in determining their learning, and it is conceivable that supervisors and managers will become their coaches. As things continue to change more rapidly, there will be a real need for staff in every organization to become professional learners. Metacognition— the awareness of one's own thought and learning processes—will be a key skill that separates high and low performers in organizations. I hope that part of our work will involve helping workers learn about learning, and develop skills to be deliberate in their learning.

In this new world, I can't help but think the notion of workplace learning will transition from a model of delivery (such as delivering a class whether it be in a classroom or online) to a model of access— where we more or less create portals for workers to retrieve learning on their terms, much like the electronic program guide on your TV. "I need help on how to give feedback in half an hour to a young member of staff who is resistance to feedback," your future learners will think. "Let's see what content I can access to prepare for this."

How the Trainer's Role Will Evolve

What does all this mean for trainers? If organizations demand new and different things, and the training department (or whatever we will call it) shifts in its focus, what will a trainer's job look like? What skills will tomorrow's trainers need to be successful? What should you be thinking about developing? If you're a learning executive, what skill sets should you be encouraging your teams to develop? I think trainers will need six core skill clusters.

Business Partnership Skills

Trainers will be partners with the business or client, helping them achieve their goals, rather than subject matter experts who simply deliver content. They'll intimately know the organization's work, priorities, workflows, markets, stresses, and the challenges making it hard for them to achieve their goals. They'll map business needs to learning solutions. This will give them the knowledge to predict future learning needs. They'll be savvy enough to navigate the corporate ecosystem, being able to identify key stakeholders and influencers. They'll have financial literacy and know how to read a P&L statement, understand basic cashflow, and understand systems theory and how change in an organization leads to performance. If they're internal, this knowledge will be deeper. Internal trainers should be able to describe the company's annual business goals and how every aspect of training supports them. If they're external, they'll be adept at quickly getting up to speed on these matters. External trainers should know how their contract supports the organization's mission. Relationship building will be a key part of this.

Performance Analysis Skills

Trainers will assess learners' performance and design specific solutions to help them transition from novice to expert. They will need skills to conduct this analysis clinically. At the moment, gut feel is commonly used to dispense with this help. Trainers will need to master the language of skills and expertise, possibly using models such as the Dreyfus and Dreyfus seven-step model. Solutions will extend beyond the classroom to mentoring, on-the-job training, and other approaches that may not require the training department. They will have conversations where learning solutions can be mapped to results. They'll also need to facilitate or recommend evidence-based approaches to building these skills.

Facilitation Skills

Trainers have used their facilitation skills as a core part of their role for as long as I can remember. However, the skills were more often directed toward the classroom. What will change in the future is that facilitation will transcend the classroom from large groups to small groups to individual coaching. Shifting between these environments will be a key skill of its own. Critical to this will be drawing on evidence-based techniques and avoiding myths such as learning styles and left-right brain theory. They will need to be very good at each task and possess advanced emotional intelligence (EQ) skills. This will require a deep knowledge of memory and cognition and how to motivate people to engage in deliberate practice. This may seem controversial—I often wonder if the separation between the roles of a trainer and coach is helpful, despite the separate allowing the concept of coaching to further evolve. Today training and coaching are seen differently, but shouldn't the seasoned facilitator be able to work seamlessly between the two?

Digital Content Creation and Curation Skills

Trainers have been making content forever. Forty years ago, it was acetates and photocopies. Today it's online resources and slide decks. The concept of trainer as a content creator isn't new. What's new is the modalities and platforms trainers need to provide content through. Trainers will need the skills to churn out digital content to support remote learners and provide performance support that looks professional and polished. Whether it's a video, an audio podcast, or an interactive app, they will be tasked with making content that's engaging and expected to be able to do it fast. The quality will need to be consistently good. The days are numbered when trainers can knock out simple screen captures with voice-overs recorded on headset microphones. Trainers will curate external content that supports learners. Tomorrow's learning professional will be a media producer and need solid skills in planning, structuring, and producing professional media content following professional standards, not just winging it. We can see media production skills creeping into job descriptions for trainers already. They will also need a basic understanding of virtual reality, augmented reality, and the Internet of Things.

Emotional Intelligence Skills

It goes without saying that any job should have EQ skills as a requirement. But talent professionals are in the people business, so it is incumbent on us to have a super high level of people skills. If we can't manage conflict or constructively have difficult conversations, we're probably in the wrong game. If we don't know how to motivate and inspire, perhaps this is not the job for us. In the future, EQ skills will continue to be critical to our success.

Learning Evangelism

The final cluster of skills is promotion, and I talked about this in chapter 8. Because budgets are under constant scrutiny, trainers will be charged with educating stakeholders about the value of learning, how it maps to business objectives, and how it leads to business results. Part of this will be helping managers become talent nurturers themselves. Some of it will be eradicating the negative stereotypes that still exist about training. But more important, we need to be public affairs officers for the work we do, the work that colleagues do, and the successes our client achieves with us. I haven't met any learning executive who has put together a workshop on promotional skills for trainers. I know I certainly didn't when I was in corporate and in hindsight wish I had.

Building These Skills
Trainers will move seamlessly between accessing these skills clusters. Their work will be a balancing act between meeting business needs and individual learner's needs. Only when that balance is found will they be successful.

The Bigger Context
If you've tracked even half of what thought leaders have said about the future of our profession in blog posts and at conferences over the past five or 10 years, you'll probably think these are safe predictions. But as we discussed earlier, they won't happen in a vacuum. Changes in technology, regulation, societal values, and politics will affect them. We don't have time to go into all these, but I do want to touch on the big subject everyone talks about, technology.

My first inclination is to think that technology will change, but what we use it for will not. For example, people read maps, took snapshots on cameras, phoned restaurants for reservations, and checked into flights over counters at airports a decade ago. Today many use smartphone apps for these tasks. In fact, they use apps for thousands of activities from time management to translating time zone differences. We're doing the same things, just using convenient apps.

So will we see that sort of thing play out with robots? Some media reports have suggested that robots will rob millions of people of middle management jobs. Others argue that they'll work seamlessly with humans—in *Forbes,* Alex Knapp (2015) predicted one of the jobs of the future will be training robots to work with humans. Still others raise ethical concerns about their influence—will they one day take over the world and rule humans? I think that it's safe to assume we'll still be doing the same stuff: helping organizations perform better by providing development solutions that draw on learning fundamentals we discussed in chapter 2. Perhaps it's likely that robots might clean the whiteboard for us, bring the coffee, and help us demonstrate certain skills. But we'll certainly be using different methods to help learners wherever they exist in the ecosystem.

How about artificial intelligence (AI)? It's already changed life in fundamental ways, such as with voice recognition systems that major brands use to triage calls to call centers and Amazon predicting what books or products might interest you. But in the future, AI in the form of machine learning will likely play a big role in healthcare, accounting, marketing, and other industries. Could many of the consulting and diagnostic services a talent professional provides be ultimately performed by a more sophisticated version of Siri? Imagine a gap analysis conducted for a manager, via an app on her phone, that then recommends an external facilitator based on a database fed from LinkedIn. Yes, this could change what work we do.

But the future of implants is what has me most quizzical about the future. Like AI and robots, medical implants have been around for a long time, such as pacemakers and bionic ears. But now, microchips that store data, such as personal information, are being injected into the soft tissue between the thumb and index finger of people working for certain companies. The chips have an antenna to connect to outside devices such as security access to a building or a cash register at a company cafeteria. Orwellian? They're popular in Sweden, and some companies in the United States have offered implants to staff so they don't need to pull out their wallet when they buy lunch; they just wave their hand over a black box.

The technology in these chips has very limited range, so the thought of a spy hacking your personal information from the other side of the room is still a long way off. But how long? And what else could be stored in these little microchips? A slide deck? Video content for use in a classroom that wirelessly connects to a projector in the ceiling? There are all sorts of alarmist predictions about such implants and I confess, the idea of having data under my thumb that other people could read scares me a lot. And I'm not the type to wear a tinfoil hat. Some in the medical profession counter my concern with inherent benefits. It could save lives. For example, say a patient with a pre-existing medical issue arrives unconscious in the ER. Doctors could quickly get his blood type and other pertinent medical issues, saving valuable time and money conducting tests. I wonder how this would work in the training room?

Storing data isn't the only purpose for implants. This is where things are getting very interesting. Scientists are currently researching devices that can be implanted in the brain to increase memory capacity and perform other functions. There is still a long way to go before this becomes a reality, but this is what I think would have the most profound effect on workplace learning. As we've discussed throughout this book, learning is a cognitive process around the function of memory. Will we merely copy and paste new skills and knowledge into their brains?

I struggle to see how this will ultimately come together. But one thing is clear: If we're to be successful in the future, we need to be agile and constantly learning new things. So much is going to change in the coming years that learning is going to be an indispensable skill. As learning professionals, we, more than anyone, understand what needs to happen if we're to learn a new skill or piece of knowledge. This gives us a key advantage in future-proofing our careers. But are we actively doing so? What are we doing to ensure our understanding is always up-to-date? What are we doing in terms of deliberate practice to remember what we are learning? How are we applying it? The more skillful we ourselves are at learning, the better we'll respond, rather than react, to changes.

Earlier I listed some of the key skills that I think trainers and talent development professionals need to be successful in the future. I believe that success in these roles is dependent on maintaining and deepening knowledge in the areas of learning science, organizational dynamics, and digital technology. We need to be the people in our organizations who have evidence-based solutions to help staff learn the new skills they need. We need to understand the organization so well that we know how to support leaders in developing talent. And we need a robust knowledge of digital technology so we're ready when everything falls into place. These areas of knowledge will help us offer laser-focused facilitation, business analysis, and curated or newly created digital media content.

Which begs the question, what are you doing to future proof yourself? It's easy for us to feel helpless, as if we're waiting for the future to unfold, hoping we have a place in it. But as Shakespeare said, it's not in the stars to hold our destiny, but in ourselves. How are you staying current with the latest studies in learning science? What organizations are you tracking to see how they disrupt conventional wisdom on making money, building products, or hiring talent? What are you reading to stay abreast of digital technology, such as AI or embedded tech, to get a sense for how it will change work? And how are you critically reflecting on what others are saying—especially those who confidently predict something, knowing their predictions could be forgotten in 10 years' time?

Those Sunsets in the Caribbean

No one really knows what the future is like. Certainly not with the precision we'd want. But I do think we're in for an exciting ride. And I think we know enough to be discerning when planning our own development to future proof ourselves and help create our own small part of the future. Talent development professionals will have a front-row seat to many of the changes. Heck, we may even be some of those changes because we hold unique positions of influence. Which makes me think, perhaps I might put off those beach sunsets for a while, because the next decade is going to be fascinating. In fact, I'll go out on a limb and make the safest prediction I can think of: My wife and I won't be living it large in the Caribbean anytime in the next 10 years. Alas. We'll be here somewhere in the United States as the future builds itself. But rather than merely watch or predict it, I want to help build it, which brings us full circle, back to learning and talent.

I'll leave you with some parting thoughts:

As long as we cling to the old notion of trainers delivering content, we'll be judged as theater performers. I'm confident that if that's how learning worked, we trainers could and would be the greatest presenters, making people happy to sit back and watch. But that's not how people learn, and so the presenter mindset will only stroke our own egos, while people leave our workshops, return to their desks, and forget much of what we presented.

Those of us who let go of the keynote mindset and adopt a physical therapist lens, which focuses truly on helping the learners meet their business goals by doing the work of learning, will see them achieve remarkable results. These achievements will only reinforce the value that we bring to our organizations. And over the coming years we're going to see many changes in how we help people learn, but what won't change is that we need to have the learner doing the work of firing those neurons.

It's truly a noble task, what trainers do. Whether we're in Moscow winging it because the client briefed us on the wrong training need, or sitting with our boss working out a way to deliver learning to a division of the company that's notoriously ambivalent about training, what we do is critical. When the learner is at the heart of what we do, and the work our organizations do is our focus, we can earn our keep. And we help the learners earn their salaries, too, and progress in their careers. We help organizations become successful. When learners allow us to help them, it's an enormous privilege that I hope none of us ever takes lightly.

REFERENCES

Baker, M. 2015. "Over Half of Psychology Studies Fail Reproducibility Test." *Nature* News, August 27. www.nature.com/news/over -half-of-psychology-studies-fail-reproducibility-test-1.18248.

Biech, E. 2015. *101 More Ways to Make Training Active.* Hoboken, NJ: Wiley.

Biech, E. 2017. *The Art and Science of Training.* Alexandria, VA: ATD Press.

Brown, P.C., H.L Roediger III, and M.A. McDaniel. 2014. *Make It Stick: The Science of Successful Learning.* Cambridge, MA: Harvard University Press.

Chalmers, A.F. 2013. *What's This Thing Called Science?,* 4th ed. Queensland, Australia: University of Queensland Press.

Clark, R.C. 2015. *Evidence-Based Training Methods: A Guide for Training Professionals,* 2nd Edition. Alexandria, VA: ATD Press.

Ericsson, K.A., R.T. Krampe, and C. Tesch-Romer. 1993. "The Role of Deliberate Practice in the Acquisition of Expert Performance." *Psychological Review* 100(3): 363–406.

Fryer, B. 2006. "Sleep Deficit: The Performance Killer." *Harvard Business Review,* October. https://hbr.org/2006/10/sleep-deficit-the-performance-killer.

Gilbert-Ouimet, M., et al. 2018. "Adverse Effect of Long Work Hours on Incident Diabetes in 7065 Ontario Workers Followed for 12 Years." *BMJ Open Diabetes Research and Care* 6(1): e000496.

Gladwell, M. 2011. *Outliers: The Story of Success.* New York: Little, Brown and Company.

HeartMath. 2014. "Stress and Cognitive Decline." Science of the Heart blog, January 21. www.heartmath.org/articles-of-the-heart/science-of-the-heart/stress-and-cognitive-decline.

Heath, C., and D. Heath. 2007. *Made to Stick: Why Some Ideas Survive and Others Die.* New York: Random House.

Hunter, M. 2011. "A Microscopic Look at Hotel Hygiene." CNN the Upgrade, February 25. www.cnn.com/2011/TRAVEL/02/25/hotel.hygiene/index.html.

Jones, J.M. 2013. "In U.S., 40% Get Less Than Recommended Amount of Sleep." Gallup News, December 19. https://news.gallup.com/poll/166553/less-recommended-amount-sleep.aspx.

Kelly, D. 2013. "What Is a Learning Ecosystem?" TWIST, the eLearning Guild blog, November 18. http://twist.elearningguild.net/2013/11/what-is-a-learning-ecosystem.

Kelly, D. 2015. "Exploring the Learning and Performance Ecosystem—Resources Shared at #ATDTK." David Kelly blog, January 16. http://davidkelly.me/2015/01/exploring-learning-performance-ecosystem-resources-shared-atdtk.

Kessler, R.C. 2011. "Insomnia and the Performance of US Workers: Results From the America Insomnia Survey." *Sleep* 34(9): 1161-1171.

Kivimäki, M., et al. 2015. "Long Working Hours and Risk of Coronary Heart Disease and Stroke: A Systematic Review and Meta-Analysis of published and Unpublished Data for 603,838 Individuals." *Lancet* 386 (10005): 1739-46.

Kivimäki, M., et al. 2017. "Long Working Hours as a Risk Factor for Atrial Fibrillation: A Multi-Cohort Study." *European Heart Journal* 38(4): 2621-28.

Knapp, A. 2015. "The Job of the Future Is Training Robots to Work With Humans." *Forbes,* May 25. www.forbes.com/sites/alexknapp /2015/05/06/how-businesses-are-teaching-robots-new-tricks.

Loehr, J., and T. Schwartz. 2005. *The Power of Full Engagement: Managing Energy, Not Time, Is the Key to High Performance and Personal Renewal.* New York: Free Press.

Lucas, R. 2016. "Defining Learning Ecosystems." Fredrickson Learning blog, April 20. https://fredricksonlearning.com/defining-learning -ecosystems.

Mautz, S. 2017. "Psychology and Neuroscience Blow-Up the Myth of Effective Multitasking." *Inc.,* May 11. www.inc.com/scott-mautz /psychology-and-neuroscience-blow-up-the-myth-of-effective -multitasking.html.

National Sleep Foundation. n.d. "How Lack of Sleep Impacts Cognitive Performance and Focus." How Sleep Works blog. www.sleepfoundation.org/how-sleep-works/how-lack-sleep-impacts -cognitive-performance-and-focus.

Pattison, K. 2008. "Worker, Interrupted: The Cost of Task Switching." *Fast Company,* July 28. www.fastcompany.com/944128/worker -interrupted-cost-task-switching.

Phillips, J.J., and P.P. Phillips. 2015. *High-Impact Human Capital Strategy: Addressing the 12 Major Challenges Today's Organizations Face.* New York: AMACOM.

Pruitt, J. 2017. "3 Top Traits of Effective Agile Leaders." *Inc.,* June 14. www.inc.com/jeff-pruitt/3-ways-to-leverage-agile-leadership.html.

Quinn, C.N. 2018. *Millennials, Goldfish & Other Training Misconceptions: Debunking Learning Myths and Superstitions.* Alexandria, VA: ATD Press.

Robinson, J. 2013. "Three-Quarters of Your Doctor Bills Are Because of This." *Huffington Post* blog, May 22. www.huffingtonpost.com /joe-robinson/stress-and-health_b_3313606.html.

Seagraves, T. 2004. *Quick! Show Me Your Value.* Alexandria, VA: ASTD Press.

Smith, O. 2018. "Have Plane Seats Really Shrunk—and Which Is the Worst Airline on Earth for Legroom?" *The Telegraph,* March 29. www.telegraph.co.uk/travel/comment/plane-seats-legroom -shrunk-worst-airline.

Syed, M. 2011. *Bounce: Mozart, Federer, Picasso, Beckham, and the Science of Success.* New York: Harper Perennial.

Wilcox, C. 2011. "Mythbusting 101: Organic Farming > Conventional Agriculture." *Scientific American,* July 18. https://blogs.scientific american.com/science-sushi/httpblogsscientificamericancomscience -sushi20110718mythbusting-101-organic-farming-conventional -agriculture.

Zeveloff, J. 2013. "The 10 Happiest and Healthiest Cities In America." *Business Insider,* March 27. www.businessinsider .com/happiest-and-healthiest-cities-in-america-2013-3.

ABOUT THE AUTHOR

Jonathan Halls woke up one morning and realized he'd been doing workplace training for more than 25 years, in more than 25 countries, with people of more than 25 nationalities. In those years, it seems, more than 25,000 things have happened to him in the classroom that no one ever told him to expect. Hence this book. Now he runs workshops for trainers and speaks at conferences around the globe.

Formerly the head of the BBC's prestigious television production training department in the UK, Jonathan's now based in Washington, D.C., where he runs Trainer Mojo, a company that delivers evidence-based train-the-trainer workshops and advanced programs for learning professionals. Author of the profession's leading book on video for trainers and a contributor to various industry journals, he is also an adjunct professor at George Washington University.

Jonathan is skeptical of fads and buzzwords, often wondering if we've lost the art of critical reflection. But then he gets excited because he keeps bumping into humble trainers who are doing amazing things by applying evidence-based learning practice. Having worked in most facets of learning as a trainer, training manager, learning executive, and contractor, Jonathan has also earned his bread and butter in non-training jobs, including talk show host, journalist, and communications manager. He has both a bachelor's and master's in adult learning. In his spare time, he likes cooking, drinking wine, playing the piano, and making furniture. Yes, he really makes furniture.

Jonathan is author of *Rapid Video Development for Trainers* (2012), *Memory and Cognition in Learning* (2013), *Rapid Media Development for Trainers* (2016), *Video Script Writing* (2014), and *Learning Science: A Pocket Book for Workplace Trainers and Talent Professionals* (2019). He has written numerous articles for professional magazines including *TD* magazine, *Learning Solutions* magazine, and *The HR Observer*. Visit www.trainermojo.com to sign up for his weekly learning helpline.